ACKNOWLEDGEMEN

This book represents the synthesis of many years of research, work experience, teaching, and consulting. It integrates our best thinking from our ten-book *Innovative Leadership* series, hundreds of research papers, and doctoral research, all updated with additional insights. We also added Artificial Intelligence information from a broad range of sources, understanding that this content is evolving daily.

We would first like to acknowledge our employers and former employers, patients, students, clients, and colleagues for providing practical opportunities to learn and build strong skills in leadership, consulting, organizational change, large-scale systems change, strategic thinking, and technology. It was this solid foundation that allowed us to create this methodology.

As a theoretical foundation, we worked with or studied many thought leaders in leadership development, developmental psychology, and integral theory. A few of the theoretical giants on whose hard work we built the Innovative Leadership and Organizational Transformation models include Susanne Cook-Grueter, Ph.D., Belinda Gore, Ph.D., Terri O'Fallon, Ph.D., Wiley W. Souba, Jr., MD, ScD, M.B.A., and Ken Wilber. These leaders shared their theories and ongoing guidance and encouragement, creating a solid framework that is comprehensive and theoretically grounded.

We give further thanks to the following:

Researchers, practitioners, authors, and thought leaders whose work contributed directly to this book, including Mary Crossan, M.B.A., Ph.D., Paul MacPherson Chair in Strategic Leadership at the Ivey Business School, Western University; James K. Stoller, M.D., M.S., Chairman, Education Institute, Jean Wall Bennett Professor of Medicine at the Cleveland Clinic, & Samson Global Leadership Chair; Mark Palmer, Managing Partner, Hire Direction; and Steve Terrell, Ed.D, President, Aspire Consulting, Inc.

We're also indebted to all the friends and colleagues who served as constant cheerleaders and readers, made suggestions, listened to stories and dreams about the book, and helped make it come to fruition — as well as the teachers, trainers, and mentors who taught us how to lead — and when to follow.

Our families provided continued support and encouragement and inspired us to be thoughtful and dedicated to working and contributing to the world meaningfully.

Finally, we thank publisher and friend Guy Du Plessis; graphic design and layout firm Creative Spot; illustrator Virpi Oinonen; and the reviewers, endorsers, thought partners, and countless others who spent untold hours making this possible. You are all appreciated so very much!

First Published by
Phronesis Publishing (Pty) Ltd
www.phronesispublishing.com
info@phronesispublishing.com

Innovative Leadership & Followership
in the Age of AI: A Guide to Creating
Your Future as Leader, Follower, and
AI Ally

1ST Edition

ISBN: 978-0-7961-1689-5

Cover Design and Layout by
Creative Spot - www.creativespot.com

Illustrations by Virpi Oinonen
www.businessillustrator.com

TABLE OF CONTENTS

" *It is not the critic who counts; not the man who points out how the strong man stumbles, or where the doer of deeds could have done them better.*

The credit belongs to the man who is actually in the arena, whose face is marred by dust and sweat and blood; who strives valiantly; who errs, who comes short again and again, because there is no effort without error and shortcoming; but who does actually strive to do the deeds; who knows great enthusiasms, the great devotions; who spends himself in a worthy cause; who at the best knows, in the end, the triumph of high achievement, and who at the worst, if he fails, at least fails while daring greatly, so that his place shall never be with those cold and timid souls who neither knows victory nor defeat.

U.S. President Theodore Roosevelt

April 23, 1910

FOREWORD

by Neil Sahota

Meet Lynn, a Customer Service Representative at ACME Corporation. Lynn's manager is Riley, an AI (artificial intelligence) bot. Riley listens to all Lynn's calls in real-time and provides instantaneous guidance and performance feedback. Lynn is part of the next-generation workforce and appreciates Riley's management style because Riley provides the deep engagement and constant interaction that Lynn craves to feel as a contributing member of the team. Now, meet Pat, the human manager of Riley and a team comprised of humans and AI bots. As a second-line manager, Pat has management and leadership responsibilities to the downline reports to direct their work and inspire them towards ACME corporate goals. It is not easy when people have a variety of motivators and AI bots, well, none save what they have been trained to do.

Sound like an exciting future?

Surprise, surprise, this is very much the present. Everything described already exists. And, yes, AI systems are directing human work...and yes, human managers are directing AI "employees."

We live in a time of rapid change, with tools that can cause a massive impact (both positive and negative). As a result, traditional leadership styles are too slow and disengaging for the workforce. Moreover, with the increasing pressure to build innovative teams and intrapreneurial cultures, leaders face the dual challenge of honing their skills and teams without many proven models to rely upon. To make life even more complicated, today's leadership is faced with learning to manage and lead in a post-COVID world that requires managers to assess performance and steward employee well-being. Furthermore, leaders are also expected to be JEDI champions: facilitators of justice, equity, diversity, and inclusion in the workplace.

This is why we need books like this one on Innovative Leadership. Historically, people were thrust into management and leadership roles based on their non-supervisory work performance. More rigorous leadership programs were developed as business advanced to help prepare people for this transition. However, change has outpaced the curriculum development. Today's leaders must understand the ever-evolving workforce and new transformative technological tools like artificial intelligence. Like it or not, the demands of today's employees expect you to be ready (and that includes those AI bots), and there's not a lot of time or patience for leadership to adjust and be effective.

Thankfully, while you may not need to worry about AI employees in the very near future, we do have some powerful AI and other emerging technology tools to support us as we shift into Innovative Leadership. From a data perspective, leaders and managers have many data points to assess work performance. In the case of Lynn, we have our traditional metrics of wait time, resolution time, the number of levels supported, and so forth. However, thanks to AI tools, we can also better assess customer satisfaction throughout the entire call, using the science of psychographics (psychology and personality assessment) and neurolinguistics (science of language and word choice.) More importantly, AI can assess the real-time performance of Lynn (or any other employee) as they interact with the customer. Depending on how the call progresses, the AI will provide instantaneous feedback and coaching to the employee to maximize the opportunity of a beneficial outcome for the call. That's a level most managers cannot do with a single employee, let alone an entire team. More importantly, the insight the AI provides into employee performance is the most important for a leader to gauge employee performance and maximize customer engagement.

This is just the tip of the iceberg for leadership regarding tooling. The ability for introspection and honest, constructive feedback for leaders is critical. Getting this input, though, is challenging. This is where AI presents another boon for leaders: *the honest assessment of leadership skills.* As we move forward, there isn't a single prototypical leader. We have different archetypes (the nine types of leaders as you will read in this book) based upon the ten core skills (also shared in this book.) AI tools help leaders fairly and accurately assess these capabilities. This is crucial to help us understand our strengths and weaknesses and which type of leader we are to maximize our strengths. As we understand what an innovative leader means, we also see how difficult it is to get honest feedback from our staff and colleagues. Artificial intelligence provides leadership with another trusted source of information (beyond employee performance) to help us become innovative leaders.

Moreover, as we look to the future of work, it's not only enterprises wondering what the jobs and leaders of tomorrow must bring to the table. Government agencies are investing heavily to adjust their workforce development programs accordingly. Singapore has created the *TechSkills Accelerator (TeSA) initiative and AI Apprenticeship Program (AIAP)* to provide the existing and future workforce with hands-on experience for these jobs of tomorrow. Canada has adopted Canada's AI Augmented Workforce for their future work plan. The State of California has adopted an AI roadmap. The core tenants require full integration of AI skill development in K-12 and higher education curricula and a mandate to integrate AI tools to provide public services, including labor management and workforce development. That's why management and leadership must be the first to understand and adapt to these changes because they will be the ones to lead the upcoming transformation of work.

To start leading your human and machine workforce soon, the leaders must master ten critical skills. This book will share how to do that and essential frameworks to factor in contextual understanding and situational analysis. In essence, this book will serve as your sherpa as you enter the new world of Innovative Leadership. AI will be your leadership concierge so that you can maximize your effectiveness and support your employees in realizing their peak performance.

INTRODUCTION

This text is the eleventh book in the *Innovative Leadership* series. It is based on the authors' collective experiences as consultants, practitioners, educators, and scholars. It's also a response to input from readers of the previous books to focus on the essential information regarding Innovative Leadership and how the elements of Innovative Leadership apply to the challenges and opportunities we all face in our professional and personal lives.

Since writing those first books, we have come to appreciate the importance of addressing both leadership **and** followership in maximizing individual, team, and organizational success. Without followers, there are no leaders. Without understanding, respecting, motivating, and engaging followers, it is impossible to execute Innovative Leadership. We've also realized that leading and following are not absolutes: there are times when we each can — and should — lead, and there are times when we each can — and should — follow, depending on the situation, personnel, resources, and context.

True to the spirit of innovation in our title, the burst of Artificial Intelligence in the workplace prompted our decision to use AI as a tool in the preparation of this book. We also wanted to model something all leaders will soon grapple with: leading a workforce that includes both humans and machines, whether on the factory floor or in C-suite offices.

We instructed AI to draw from our previous books, especially 2021's *Innovative Leadership for Health Care*, along with several *Innovating Leadership: Co-Creating Our Future* podcast episodes. We had AI summarize the content in a style and format that we identified as relevant and optimal for mid-level leaders. With that summary as a draft, we carefully reviewed, edited, and revised each chapter for accuracy to ensure that the content conveyed our intent. We also added more recent information that did not appear in our previous books. Because we believe that AI and its relevance to leadership will continue to evolve, we included a separate chapter focused on ways leaders can — and **must** — adapt to the evolving AI ecosystem and other workplace technologies yet to be imagined. The result? The clear presentation of the essential elements of Innovative Leadership and Followership you now hold in your hands. We hope you'll agree as you read on!

The list below presents exceptional leaders' top ten skills and behaviors needed for leading a workforce of humans and AI:

1. **Communication**

   Outstanding leaders continually focus on essential leadership skills that involve relating to others — communication, collaboration, negotiation, facilitation, social influence, change management, and active listening.

2. **Growth Mindset**

   During the massive opportunities created by change, leaders must cultivate a growth mindset with curiosity, lifelong learning, and an ability to unlearn and stop doing things that no longer serve their mission.

3. **Adaptiveness**

   Notable leaders enhance their ability to anticipate change and proactively initiate aligned change initiatives. This requires building adaptiveness, resilience, and workplace agility.

4. **Emotional Intelligence**

   Because teams will need to make changes that often feel unfamiliar and uncomfortable, the most effective leaders will amplify their emotional intelligence (EQ). This includes self-awareness, self-management, relationship awareness, empathy, building trust and psychological safety, and other skills that help a leader relate to and inspire others.

5. **Abundance Mindset**

   Developing an abundance — as opposed to scarcity — mindset lets a leader reframe uncomfortable situations into opportunities. An abundance mindset is a belief that there are more than enough resources (including time and talent) to achieve goals — that, collectively, the team has the knowledge, wisdom, resources, skills, and attitude to meet the challenges ahead when they consistently act from abundance beliefs and actively create the future they want to see. They create solutions that resolve scarcity.

6. **Domain Expertise**

   Successful leaders continue to excel in their areas of domain expertise and understand the latest technological developments in those areas, from finance to medicine. Whatever the field, keeping current is vital!

7. **AI Skills**

   As artificial intelligence continues its rapid evolution, leaders (and their teams) will need to know how to leverage AI to gather useful information and get work done. The better the questions, the better AI serves the team.

8. **Analytical, Decision-Making, and Systems Thinking Skills**

   To leverage AI, leaders will need to understand and weigh its output. Strong analytical, decision-making, and systems thinking skills will help leaders with that assessment and continue to improve AI's results and its value to the organization.

9. **Creativity**

   A creative perspective and creative thinking abilities aid in identifying areas AI will not consider or developing solutions AI can't yet come up with. Knowing where to experiment with possible solutions is vital, too.

10. **Risk Awareness**

   AI presents its own risks; leaders need to understand these and continually evolve governance processes to address them.

As you read through the first few chapters, you'll learn about the seven elements of Innovative Leadership. The following table frames which of those elements apply to — and help you continue developing — each of the ten skills and behaviors you'll need to successfully bridge the gap and integrate a combined Human-AI workplace in this evolving world. As you finish each chapter, revisit this table to consider how Innovative Leadership concepts amplify your leadership ability.

As you learn more about these skills, ask yourself: How will the leadership foundation you'll forge from this book influence the ways you lead a workforce of humans and machines?

TABLE I: RELATING THE ELEMENTS OF INNOVATIVE LEADERSHIP WITH HYBRID WORKFORCE NEEDS

Skills to Lead a Hybrid (Human-AI) Workforce	Type	Perspectives	Mindset	Resilience	Skills	Context	Leader/Follower
1. COMMUNICATION and other essential leadership skills — collaboration, negotiation, facilitation, social influence, and active listening.	X	X	X		X	X	X
2. GROWTH MINDSET — curiosity, lifelong learning, and the ability to unlearn and stop doing things that no longer serve your mission.		X	X				
3. ADAPTIVENESS to anticipate change and proactively launch aligned change initiatives; build your adaptiveness, resilience, and business agility.		X	X	X	X	X	X
4. EMOTIONAL INTELLIGENCE, including self-awareness, self-management, relationship awareness, empathy, building trust and psychological safety, and other skills that help relate to and inspire others.	X	X	X	X	X	X	X
5. A MINDSET OF ABUNDANCE (versus scarcity) to reframe uncomfortable situations into opportunities.		X	X	X			
6. DOMAIN EXPERTISE and understanding the latest technological developments affecting your areas of expertise.					X	X	

Skills to Lead a Hybrid (Human-AI) Workforce	Type	Perspectives	Mindset	Resilience	Skills	Context	Leader/Follower
7. AI SKILLS to leverage the technology for useful information and to get work done.					X	X	
8. SYSTEMS THINKING, along with strong analytical, problem-solving, and decision-making skills.		X	X		X	X	
9. CREATIVE PERSPECTIVES to identify areas AI doesn't consider. Experiment with possible solutions.		X	X		X	X	
10. UNDERSTAND THE RISKS — AI presents its own risks; leaders need to understand these and continually evolve governance processes to address them.		X	X		X	X	

· CHAPTER 1 ·

What *Is* Innovative Leadership?

Leadership is a combination of being, relating, and doing.
Start your leadership journey by building self-reflection skills.

CHAPTER 1

What *Is* Innovative Leadership?

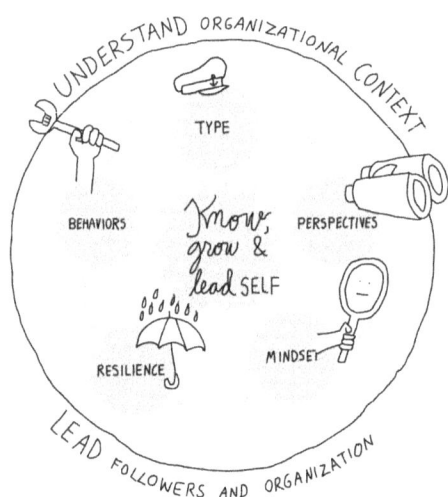

Figure 1.1: The Innovative Leadership Framework

Today's leaders significantly impact the future — their decisions and actions will ripple through the next few generations. Unfortunately, too many leaders use depreciated or outdated skills. While most of us wouldn't think of using a ten-year-old computer, many of us work with people who use the same leadership approach they had ten or even twenty-plus years ago with only mediocre results.

COVID, AI, climate change, hybrid work, politics: the world has changed in so many ways over the last few years. Leadership clearly must change with it. Organizations must redefine what effective leadership is and elevate the quality of their leaders to meet these ever-changing challenges. Innovative Leadership offers a way for you to do just that — to advance your own development as a leader and advance your organization in the process.

Technology has significantly changed what and how we lead. As leaders, we need to understand new tools and how those tools change relationships. Smartphones, for example, changed how we relate to others: texting, social media, swiping left or right, videos — almost anything but an actual conversation in a phone call! We need to understand emerging technologies, how to use and adapt to them, and how to update our thinking processes, skills, and communication styles to adapt seamlessly and effectively.

So, What *Is* Innovative Leadership?

In short, Innovative Leadership is the use of leadership research to maximize engagement, cohesiveness, and performance in your team to accomplish your organization's mission and vision. Any growth means change, but Innovative Leadership is <u>structured</u> change, helping you see and develop your unique strengths. By definition, an innovative leader is constantly learning and growing — building on their solid foundational leadership practices while learning new ones. Just as important, they **unlearn** outdated practices.

Our organizations and societies face a world that is constantly becoming more complex and faster-paced. To remain relevant (and effective!), we, as innovative leaders, need to consider the latest research, trends, and challenges. We can then determine how our individual and organizational leadership must adapt to change. Critically, we elevate our leadership to meet current *and* anticipated conditions, challenges, and opportunities. Effective Innovative Leadership also requires understanding, motivating, and engaging followers to contribute meaningfully and help us identify ways to be innovative.

Innovative leaders deliver results by blending:

1. **Strategic leadership,** which inspires people's *intentions and goals* and organizational *vision and culture;*

2. **Tactical leadership,** which influences people's *actions* and the organization's *systems and processes;* and

3. **Holistic leadership,** which aligns all core dimensions: individual intentions and action with organizational culture and systems. These are all aligned with the organization's ecosystem.

The Difference

The most effective leaders are self-aware. Self-awareness consists of internal self-awareness (i.e., awareness of our values, personality, style, strengths, biases, and so on) and external self awareness (how others perceive our values, personality, style, strengths, biases, etc.).

Innovative leaders work with others the same way conductors work with musicians in an orchestra. Everyone works together to create the product: music. The quality of the performance depends on the cohesiveness, commitment, and coordination of all orchestra members, not just their individual talents.

Conductors "orchestrate" those elements, inspiring their musicians to produce exceptional performances. Good conductors are technically skilled; brilliant conductors embody the music. The magic happens when the conductor and the musicians merge into one interconnected being, and that gestalt touches and captivates the audience.

You can conduct your team to give world-class results *every time* they perform. Innovative Leadership is the key difference between a command performance and mediocrity.

The Leader-Follower Relationship

It is important for innovative leaders to understand followership and enhance leader-follower relationships. After all, without followers, who are you leading?

You (as a leader) work with your team (the followers) to:

- Convey and embody a vision, mission, and culture to accomplish the organization's greatest potential;

- Inspire, motivate, and engage;

- Develop resources to expand organizational capacity;

- Create an environment of mutual support that maximizes value creation; and

- Develops all employees to optimize their potential.

Your team, in turn, gives its best effort to accomplish the mission in collaboration with you. *Innovative followers* are active members of the team who contribute new ideas and new approaches to achieve success for individuals, the team, and the organization as a whole. They see the highest potential of the team and its members and actively contribute to deliver that potential.

As with our music analogy, brilliant music only happens when everyone works together – listening, learning, sharing, and supporting each other; that's how legendary concerts are born. It's hardly a coincidence!

In your organization, it is important that you, as a leader, consider the needs of the followers and give every reasonable effort to enable them to thrive and deliver their best. The followers pay it forward by actively supporting the team to achieve your organization's vision and mission.

Keep this in mind: leadership and followership roles can ebb and flow, regardless of a person's title. Each of your team members (including you) might lead or follow at any given time, depending on the situation and a particular team member's knowledge, skills, abilities, and attitudes. When you build a trusting and cohesive team, you can seamlessly pass the baton to ensure success.

The Opportunity for Innovative Leadership

With the extraordinary rate of change in today's world, leaders with an obsolete perspective often unintentionally damage their organizations. At the very least, their outdated algorithms create a disadvantage with competitors.

Here's an example: according to Gallup's *State of the Global Workplace: 2023 Report*, employee engagement worldwide is very low: only 23% of employees are actively engaged in their work. This largely stems from old, disproven leader attitudes, such as a belief that socializing at work reduces productivity. In reality, forging friendships among coworkers has a significant positive impact on employee engagement. And more employee engagement results in *more productive* work!

Gallup found in 2022 that since the start of the pandemic, having a "best friend" at work has had an even more significant impact on essential outcomes — like workers' likelihood to recommend their workplace, intent to leave, and overall satisfaction. Moreover, with growing issues of anxiety and depression, best friends at work have become lifelines who provide crucial social connections, psychological safety, collaboration, and support for each other during times of change.

Innovative leaders understand how the field of leadership is evolving. They stay current on trends in employee engagement, workplace well-being, and leadership research. They encourage supportive work relationships because they understand that these relationships boost engagement and productivity while helping reduce anxiety and depression.

In short, they go beyond theory, implementing what they learn. Innovative leaders update their leadership practices to operate from the latest frameworks. Staying "leadership fresh" makes them more adaptable, their mindsets are more flexible, and they are more capable of taking calculated risks. They also understand the importance of creating a shared mutual purpose and aligning all aspects of their organizations with that purpose.

Are you ready to take the journey to develop those qualities?

There *Is* a Difference: Innovative vs. Traditional Leaders

What differentiates an innovative leader from a traditional leader? You can see their differences in this table:

TABLE 1.1: TRADITIONAL AND INNOVATIVE LEADERSHIP COMPARISON	
A TRADITIONAL LEADER	AN INNOVATIVE LEADER
Is mainly guided by a desire for personal success (and tangentially by organizational success).	Is guided by an altruistic vision of success and provides humble guidance based on performance and the value of the organization's positive impact.
Decides in a "command and control" style; thinks the leader has all the answers.	Leverages the team for answers as part of the decision-making process; knows the leader may not have all the answers, but the team can help.
Picks a direction in a "black/white" manner; tends to dogmatically stay the course.	Perceives and behaves like a scientist: identifies what questions to ask; continually experiments, measures, and tests for improvement; and continuously explores and adapts new models and approaches.
Focuses on being technically correct and in charge.	Enthusiastically curious: constantly learning and developing self and others.
Manages people by being autocratic and controlling.	Engages, motivates and inspires people through strategic focus, mentoring & coaching, and emotional & social intelligence.

A TRADITIONAL LEADER	AN INNOVATIVE LEADER
Focuses on the numbers; uses quantitative measures to drive those numbers.	Pays attention to performance, customer satisfaction, employee engagement, community impact, and cultural cohesion.
Conducts long-term planning.	Continually scans the environment for risks, opportunities, and emerging trends.

The Innovative Leadership Framework

Individuals who want to elevate their capabilities and update their leadership algorithm can use the *Innovative Leadership Framework*. This framework guides you through a self-discovery process to identify your own purpose and values. Understanding vision and values is the foundation of leadership, so first, we assess and reflect on who we are as a person *and* as a leader through multiple lenses. Then, we can create a plan to develop ourselves in the context of our organization. Finally, we lead — more effectively — using our newly enhanced leadership algorithm, supporting our organization to deliver its mission.

There are seven elements to the Innovative Leadership Framework which we will discuss in subsequent chapters (see Figure 1.1):

The 5 Inner Circles (Encompassing the Elements of Leading Oneself)

- **Leader *Type*** reflects your core predispositions, traits, and attitudes. This impacts who you are as a leader, how you respond to stress, and how people will experience your leadership.

- **Developmental *Perspective*** is your "meaning-making," or how you make sense of experiences. The algorithm you use to make sense of the world influences your thoughts and actions.

- ***Mindset*** is a set of beliefs, attitudes, and assumptions that create your mental framework which guides your thoughts and actions.

- ***Resilience*** is your ability to remain flexible and focused, adapting in the face of change. Your organization can be resilient, too, helping it achieve its strategic goals.

    ⌐ *Skills* **and Behaviors** are your specific abilities and the actions you take. They often involve both technical competencies and interpersonal abilities.

The Outer Circle (Encompassing the Elements of Leading Others)

    ⌐ *Organizational Context* **and Situational Analysis** are ways of understanding the interaction between yourself, company culture, your actions, the organization's systems and processes, and the broader eco-system. Balancing and aligning all those factors facilitates sustainable change.

    ⌐ *Lead Followers and Organization* is the goal! This book aims to help you with this part of the framework — to lead in an innovative, ethical, and engaging fashion. Leadership and followership happen together — like a beautiful dance, leaders and followers collaborate to support the overall mission. These roles can be fluid, and are not title based.

Leadership development starts with understanding yourself. This book helps you do exactly that: the following chapters dive into each of the elements above, so you can understand what they are and how they work. There are also reflection questions, enabling you to see those elements within yourself and develop them further. In short, you'll get the who, what, when, where, why, and how of an innovative leader and a courageous follower — and your strengths within those roles.

What Is a "Learning Mindset"?

Think of a mindset as a mental attitude that determines how you interpret and respond to situations. A *Learning* Mindset is an attitude of openness to new experiences, to believe you can and will learn, and to grow and develop from your experiences intentionally. It includes how you think about and approach opportunities. Leaders with a Learning Mindset see opportunities for learning in all aspects of their life: at work, at home, and at play. That's an obvious edge compared to people who are closed to learning!

Getting the Most from This Book

Our goal is simple: to help you become a better leader. That's why this book is designed to meet you where you are in your leadership journey: as an individual studying and developing independently; as part of a small group that gets together to discuss the lessons; or as a member of a larger group working with an instructor, facilitator, consultant, mentor, or coach. Though this book was written with mid-level leaders in mind, we believe that this text is relevant and useful to everyone at every stage of professional and personal growth, no matter your position or title, who wants to develop their leadership knowledge, skills, and effectiveness. From student to C-suite, you'll find valuable information to help you along that journey.

As you take this opportunity to experience leadership development firsthand, consider what you hope to get out of this book. Understanding your intentions and expectations, setting your goals, and reflecting upon the relevance and applicability of the information to your life will help you achieve your desired potential.

Each chapter of the book includes reflection questions designed to guide you through the process of developing your abilities as an innovative leader. Use this sequence to get the biggest benefit:

1. ***Read Intently***

   Read the chapters thoroughly; in each one, we introduce and illustrate an integrated set of concepts for each element of our Innovative Leadership Framework.

2. ***Contemplate and Reflect***

   Think about the reflection questions at the end of each chapter. We created each one carefully so you can contemplate some meaningful, real-life implications on your leadership. You can reflect on your own or invite friends and colleagues to join you and add their thoughts.

3. ***Link Your Experience***

   As you build your understanding, you will begin noticing habits and conditioned patterns that present obvious opportunities for growth. Though you may experience personal resistance along the way, you will discover new and positive strengths. As you become more adept at using these ideas, you will find yourself increasingly engaging proactively with the concepts and increasingly able to respond to situations requiring Innovative Leadership with greater capacity.

Once you have completed the process, you will have created a plan to grow as an innovative leader.

A Note on AI in Your Leadership Journey

ALL ABOUT
AI

As you navigate the ever-changing business and leadership landscape, you must stay ahead of the curve and embrace new technologies to help you grow and evolve as a leader. The most influential tech of the 21st century so far is artificial intelligence (AI). AI refers to the ability of machines to learn and perform tasks that would typically require human intelligence, such as speech recognition, decision-making, and problem-solving.

It seems to have tendrils in nearly every aspect of modern life — and leadership is no exception. In fact, knowledge of AI will be an absolute requirement for your career: it may simply be an office tool to improve efficiency or a specialized app your company uses to make widgets. At the very least, it can dramatically help you become a better leader with custom coaching.

We believe AI will be so integral to leading in your lifetime that you'll see a special section like this one at the end of many of the following chapters. That section highlights how you can use AI in learning or executing that chapter's topic.

Test it, reject it, embrace it: how you deal with AI now can directly affect its future...and yours!

REFLECTION QUESTIONS

Consider your answers to the following questions based on the Introduction and Chapter 1:

- ⌐ What are the top five events and choices that brought you to where you currently are, both professionally and personally?

- ⌐ What stands out in the list you just made? Are there any surprises or patterns?

- ⌐ How did these events and choices contribute to buying and using this book?

- ⌐ What impact would you like to have as a leader on your group or organization? What about the impact you would like to have as a member of your current team(s), whether as a leader or a follower? How will reading this book contribute to your success?

DIVE DEEPER

Articles

Navegar por la incertidumbre y aprender con agilidad, claves en el trabajo del futuro [Navigating Complexity and Learning with Agility: Keys for the Future of Work] by David Dinwoodie, Suzie Lewis, and James Ritchie-Dunham (Harvard Duesto Business Review)

Innovative Leadership: An Ongoing Development Journey by Maureen Metcalf (Forbes)

Podcast Episodes

Innovating Leadership: Co-Creating Our Future
Season 5 Episode 48: "Evolve to Execute: Leadership Maturity"

Innovative Leadership: Co-Creating our Future
S8-Ep38: "The Power of Passion & Perseverance: Four Levels of Grit"

For our list of references and additional resources with clickable links,
go to **www.InnovativeLeadershipEssentials.com.**

CHAPTER 2

Followership and Follower Types

You need to understand your followers to lead them effectively.

CHAPTER 2

Followership and Follower Types

Followership

Leadership has been a critical aspect of organizational success for centuries, but it is increasingly important for leaders to embrace new approaches to leadership. One of these is understanding and appreciating followership. Without followers, there can be no leaders.

"Every leader is first a follower." Aristotle is said to have taught this more than 2300 years ago, but it is no less true today. This perspective can be interpreted in two different ways. It can mean that you must first be a follower before becoming a leader, or that leaders should keep foremost in mind that they are to listen to, respond to, and serve the needs of others. While other interpretations have value, it is particularly important to bear the second interpretation in mind.

Followership can be defined as the activities practiced and contributions made by individuals who are not in positions of authority, whereby they exert influence to accomplish organizational goals.

Follower Types

Followership has been addressed in some detail by several different individuals. Our co-authors, Erin Barry and Neil Grunberg, considered three approaches to followership to create an integrated model (see Figure 2.1). The Barry & Grunberg model:

1. Includes the dimension of engagement, ranging from low to high engagement, specifically: isolate, bystander, participant, activist, diehard;

2. Adds a dimension of alignment ranging from not aligned to aligned with the leader or organization, including the fact that followers require courage to support or oppose the leader or organization;

3. Indicates the importance of adapting to different situations, contexts, and individuals to achieve desired goals.

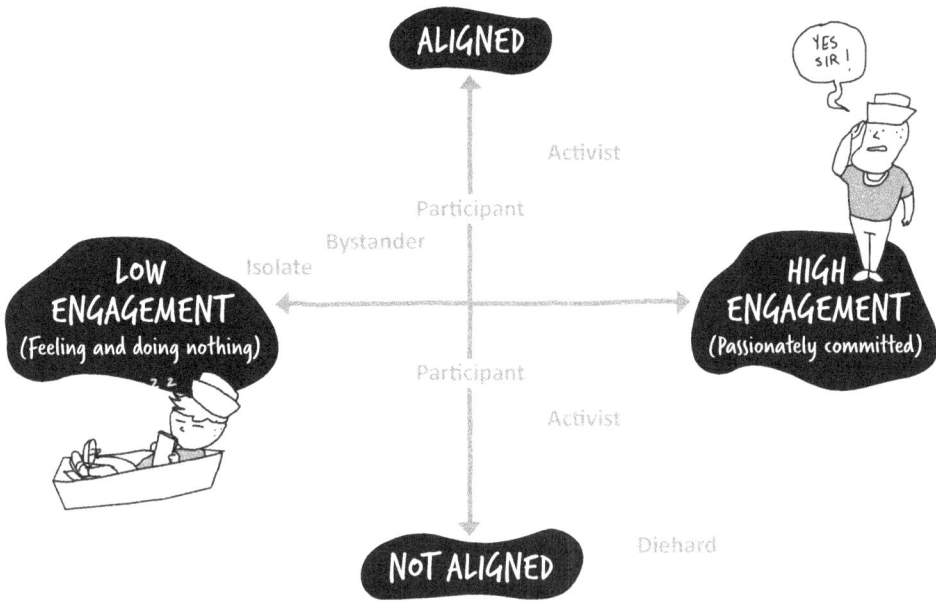

Figure 2.1: Barry & Grunberg model of followership types. Note: as follower engagement increases, they either align (and support) the leader or don't align (and oppose) the leader.

The engagement dimension is based on the work of Robert Kelley and the work of Barbara Kellerman. Kelley identified five different follower types based on two dimensions: a dimension ranging from dependent to independent thought and a dimension ranging from passive to active involvement. Kelley's five types of followers:

1. **Passive followers** are dependent on others, do not think critically, and show passive behaviors when working with themselves and others ("the sheep").

2. **Conformist followers** are dependent on others and do not think critically but are more active in their behaviors ("yes people").

3. **Alienated followers** are independent of others, can think critically, and show passive behaviors (i.e., those that have seen too much, are negative, and/or have lost their power).

4. **Effective followers** are those that are independent of others, can think critically, and show active behaviors when working with others ("the stars")

5. **Pragmatic survivors** are those that adapt to the situation ("canary in the mineshaft").

Kellerman also proposed five types of followers; these ranged along a dimension from low to high engagement, which was similar to Kelley's dimension of involvement. Kellerman's five types of followers:

1. **Isolates** are not engaged at all and are physically or psychologically absent.

2. **Bystanders** are physically present but do not engage or contribute.

3. **Participants** are present, engaged, and contribute; they are the most *common type of follower.*

4. **Activists** are present, engaged, contribute, initiate, and offer suggestions (they are the closest to innovative followers).

5. **Diehards** are present and so passionately engaged that they are "all in," no matter what.

Barry & Grunberg's consideration of courage and alignment is based on Ira Chaleff's emphasis on the importance of followers having the courage to step up and contribute or to offer comments, criticisms, and alternatives. Chaleff identified seven different ways followers can engage and be courageous by

-   *assuming responsibility* for self and the organization

-   *serving* the leader through hard work

-   *challenging* others through the sense of what is right even through discomfort or conflict

-   *participating in transformation* when change is needed

-   *taking moral action* when they have to stand against the leader

-   *speaking to the hierarchy* through awareness of the organization

-   *needing leaders to listen to followers* to be able to support conditions of courageous followership

Why Followership Is Relevant to Innovative Leadership

There are two reasons you, as an innovative leader, need to understand followership and follower types. First, leaders who understand the follower types of the members of their teams and organizations are most likely to optimize the performance of the individuals, groups, and overall organization. Second, leaders who understand their own follower type are most likely to optimize positive interactions with the members of their teams and organizations.

This understanding is particularly important during times of crisis. Leader and follower types tend to be exaggerated under stressful conditions.

When you know the follower types of your team members and organizations, you can more effectively understand, motivate, and meaningfully engage each person to everyone's mutual benefit. For example:

- With **followers who tend to be isolates or bystanders,** focus on motivating and getting them involved.

- With **followers who tend to be participants,** give clear direction and reward their actions.

- With **followers who tend to be activists or die-hards,** align them with your vision and designated mission.

Once you understand your team and have each member in their ideal role, they'll help achieve your stated goals. Those roles fluctuate depending on *you* as the leader:

- When you are confident about your vision but time is limited, you'll be well served by making **aligned followers** more prominent.

- When you desire alternative approaches and have time to consider them, it is most appropriate to make the views of those **not aligned** more prominent.

- When followers perceive your visions or activities are not in the best interest of the group, then the **followers must muster their courage** to present alternative views.

It is also important for followers to recognize when *they* need to adapt to optimize team and organizational outcomes.

FROM OUR FILES: THE POWER OF FOLLOWERSHIP

Jordan led a large organization with a multibillion-dollar budget. They are a highly evolved leader who cares deeply about their followers' success and engagement at work.

Their organization's focus changed during COVID, though. Like most leaders, Jordan needed to deliver services differently. The pandemic required rapid change, which calls for all hands to help with implementation, so Jordan created a strategy to engage all types of followers.

Jordan involved followers in helping to refine the approach to accomplishing the mission. These followers served as champions for the new approach they co-created. The champions, in turn, engaged isolates and bystanders by demonstrating the new approach worked effectively.

Jordan also carved a clear path to ensure everyone understood this was a jointly formed strategy with co-created tactics. Jordan knew — and expressed — that all followers provided input and believed in the process. This approach of soliciting input to accomplish a new mission in a new environment helped the full range of followers adapt to the changes, successfully achieving their goals.

When you understand your own follower type, you're more likely to interact positively with your team as its leader. You'll also optimize input from the team. For example, leaders who tend to be activist followers need to be aware of when to step back and listen to the input of others. Leaders who tend to be bystanders or participant followers must monitor situations to know when to step up and encourage engagement from others.

As a leader, you also need to be aware of the extent to which you are aligned (or not) with your organization and how you convey your opinions to your team members. Remember, too, that no matter how high up the leadership chain you rise, you are also a follower with regard to the system in which you operate.

Using Followership Principles to Create an Innovative Culture

In light of the importance of follower engagement to achieve goals, you must create a culture of engagement and psychological safety, build trust, and embrace accountability.

Create a culture of engagement and psychological safety. This means fostering an environment where followers feel valued, respected, and heard. You can accomplish this by encouraging open communication, valuing diverse perspectives, and creating opportunities for followers to contribute to the team and, thus, to the organization's successes.

Amy Edmonson focuses on this topic and found that cultures that have low psychological safety with low-performance standards create apathy within their organizations, whereas low psychological safety with high-performance standards creates anxiety. When psychological safety is high but performance standards are low, people are comfortable and don't need to push themselves to grow.

You want to create cultures with high psychological safety and high-performance standards to create a learning environment where people can continually experiment and grow. Psychological safety can be increased by modeling engagement with members of the team and organization while also showing understanding through active listening. It also requires you to be inclusive when interacting with others and during decision-making processes and for followers to be willing to step up and be a part of that conversation.

Build trust. You must understand the importance of building trust to become more effective and innovative. Trust is essential for building strong relationships between leaders and followers. We enter every trust relationship as both the trustor and trustee; while attempting to gain the other person's trust, we are also trying to determine how much we can trust them.

MaryJo Burchard proposed six dimensions of trust:

1. **Authenticity** — When someone can take your words and actions at face value and not feel that you are withholding information.

2. **Safety** — When someone feels safe, secure, and protected.

3. **Consistency** — When you can trust a predictable pattern of behavior.

4. **Dependability** — When someone believes you will keep your promises and confidentiality.

5. **Ownership** — When someone believes you will feel the weight of the outcomes, and when they pass it to you, you will take full responsibility.

6. **Competence** — When someone believes you have the skill needed to do what is expected.

Embrace accountability. This means taking responsibility for your actions and decisions and being willing to accept feedback and criticism. People who embrace accountability are more likely to build trust and foster engagement within their teams and organizations.

When you practice these three strategies, you create teams and organizations in which all members of the team — leaders and followers — can be courageous because they are encouraged to contribute meaningfully and innovate for the good of their teammates and organizations.

Remember that we each can lead, and we each can follow depending on the situation, mission, personnel, and resources. That is not to say that there are no positional leaders and followers within each group. It is, instead, meant to highlight that Innovative Leadership values and encourages contributions, new perspectives, and creative ideas from *all* team members, which requires leaders to "step aside" or to "follow" when appropriate, and for followers to "step up" and lead or innovate when appropriate. By understanding follower types, you can build trust, foster collaboration, and optimize contributions from all team members.

REFLECTION QUESTIONS

- What is your dominant follower type?

- Why is it important to understand others' follower types?

- How does understanding followership and follower types help you improve your ability to communicate, collaborate, and build psychological safety and trust?

- Which elements of followership should you pay particular attention to for your own development and the development of others with whom you interact professionally and socially?

- How does understanding leadership and followership help you increase your sensitivity to the unique needs of your followers during times of significant change?

DIVE DEEPER

Books

The Courageous Follower: Standing Up to and for Our Leaders by Ira Chaleff

Podcast Episodes

Innovating Leadership: Co-Creating Our Future
Season 4 Episode 9: "The Dance Between Leadership and Followership"

Innovating Leadership: Co-Creating Our Future
Season 9 Episode 3: "Courageous Followership"

Leader Type

The Enthusiast

The Loyalist

WOW, WE'RE SO CLOSE!

GET BACK IN THE BOAT! BOTH OF YOU!

FASCINATING SPECIMEN.

The Investigator

Knowing your leadership type is a foundation for leading others.

CHAPTER 3

Leader Type

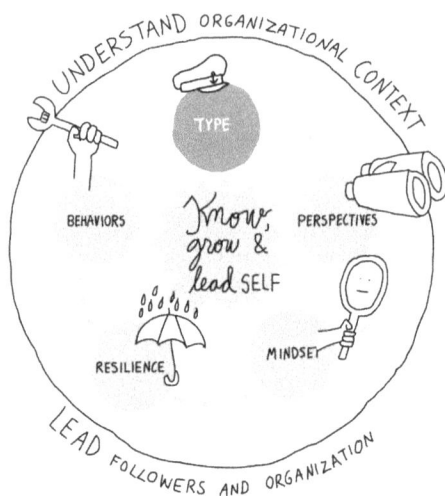

What kind of leader are you?

That's important to know: understanding yourself is the very foundation for continually adapting, developing, and growing. Despite that, it's taken a very long time to define the different types of leaders.

Historically, we viewed leaders as heroes (or villains), emphasizing particular physical attributes, knowledge and skills, charisma, commanding presence, and communication styles. This heroic individual emphasis gave way in the mid 20th Century to three leader type styles: autocratic, democratic, and laissez-faire. Then, over the past 50 years, many more leader types were identified, including adaptive, authentic, servant, shared, transactional, transformational, and, of course, innovative!

What Is Leader Type?

Leader Type reflects core predispositions, traits, and attitudes. These attributes influence who you are as a leader, how you respond to stress, and how people experience your leadership. This understanding, as with the ancient Greek adage — "Know thyself"— is essential because it provides insight into your "default" attitudes and behaviors, allowing you to adapt appropriately to each situation and the team members involved.

It significantly shapes your leadership effectiveness — but how can you know which Leader Type describes you best?

We recommend a two-pronged approach: self-reflection and objective assessment.

From taking a walk to clear your head to mindful meditation, there are many methods for self-reflection. Looking inside yourself and examining your inner makeup enables you to function in a highly grounded way rather than operating *only* from your innate biases, which inevitably lead to uninformed, reflexive, or unconscious decision-making. While biases come in many forms, we focus on personality-related biases in the area of Leader Type.

There are several valuable tools to help determine leader types, including the Enneagram, Eysenck Personality Inventory, Eysenck Personality Questionnaire, Minnesota Multiphasic Personality Inventory (MMPI), Myers Briggs Type Indicator (MBTI), Revised NEO Personality Inventory (NEO-PI-R), and True Colors.

Using the Enneagram Assessment to Build Leadership Effectiveness

We'll focus on the Enneagram assessment as an example of a Leader Type assessment. While the Enneagram assessment is a tool for building leadership effectiveness, it is one tool among many. Depending on individual needs and circumstances, other tools and strategies may be more appropriate.

The Enneagram is a system of nine interconnected personality types, each with its own strengths, weaknesses, motivations, and levels of health. By identifying your Enneagram type, you gain insight into your leadership style and how to use it more effectively.

The Enneagram assessment can help you:

- **Understand your strengths and weaknesses as a leader.** The Enneagram points to your core motivations and fears, which opens awareness of your strengths and weaknesses as a leader. This self-awareness helps you harness your strengths and work on your areas of growth.

- **Identify areas for personal growth and development.** Each Enneagram type has a path of integration (growth) and disintegration (stress). By being aware of these paths, you can actively work towards your healthier state and be wary of behaviors that may surface under stress.

- **Develop a more nuanced understanding of team dynamics** and how to lead diverse teams effectively — this helps you create an environment that plays to the collective strengths, values, and motivations of the group.

- **Know your followers' types.** You'll have a broader perspective on what drives them, so you better understand, motivate, and communicate with diverse individuals.

- **Communicate effectively.** Different Enneagram types prefer to receive information in different ways; you can tailor your communication for maximum impact, and better motivation.

- **Identify your own preferred leadership style.** Knowing how you gravitate as a leader also gives you insight into how others might receive it. You can refine your approach to better serve your followers.

The Nine Enneagram Types

You are unique. But understanding all nine types provides a valuable framework for understanding not just yourself but the different leaders and followers around you.

Type One: The Perfectionist

As leaders, Perfectionists are often driven and conscientious, with a strong sense of responsibility and a desire for order and efficiency. They strive for high standards in themselves and others (hence the Type label), and can be very detail-oriented. On the other hand, they may struggle with delegation, preferring control over the work, and may be very critical of their team's performance *and* their own.

Type Two: The Helper

Helpers are often empathetic and supportive leaders, with a strong desire to help their followers succeed. They tend to be very good at building relationships and creating a positive team culture, but may need help setting boundaries and saying no to others. They may also avoid conflict, sometimes resulting in unresolved issues and tension within the team.

Type Three: The Achiever

Achiever leaders are often highly ambitious and goal-oriented, with a strong desire to succeed. They may be very focused on achieving results and highly competitive, pushing their team members to excel. They may need help slowing down and balancing achieving their own goals at the expense of other vitals, such as team culture or work-life balance.

Type Four: The Individualist

As leaders, Individualists are often highly creative and innovative, with a strong desire to forge something unique and meaningful. They may be very attuned to the emotions of their team members and very supportive of their followers' individuality. However, they may struggle with accepting criticism and be highly sensitive, sometimes impacting their ability to lead effectively.

Type Five: The Investigator

An Investigator leader is often a highly knowledgeable expert who wants to understand complex concepts and systems. They tend to be highly analytical and very independent; due to their preference for working alone or in small groups, they may feel disconnected from their team members. They may struggle with communication and explaining complex concepts to others.

Type Six: The Loyalist

Loyalist leaders are often exceedingly responsible and dependable, firmly loyal to their followers and their organization. However, they may be very risk-averse, preferring to stick to what is safe and reliable rather than taking chances on new ideas. They may struggle with decision-making and seek reassurance from others before deciding.

Type Seven: The Enthusiast

With the leadership mantle, Enthusiasts are often energetic and highly creative, with a strong desire to explore new ideas and opportunities. They may be very good at inspiring their team members and keeping the work environment exciting and dynamic. However, they may need help with follow-through and staying focused on a particular task or project.

Type Eight: The Challenger

In leadership positions, Challengers are often highly assertive and decisive. They want to lead their team members to succeed. They may excel at making tough decisions and pushing their team members to achieve their goals, but may struggle to delegate tasks to others. Challengers sometimes come across as overly controlling or aggressive.

Type Nine: The Peacemaker

Rounding out the types, Peacemakers are often empathetic and patient leaders, with a need to create a harmonious work environment. They may be very good at mediating conflicts and finding common ground between team members. Peacemakers may need help asserting their needs and boundaries; they sometimes avoid conflict at the expense of addressing critical issues within the team.

Each of these types has unique characteristics, strengths, and weaknesses that define how we approach leadership. It is important to note that leader type is not about labeling or categorizing individuals. Instead, it is about *understanding* the complex and nuanced characteristics, preferences, and predispositions that inform how we lead.

Why Is Leader Type Important?

Everyone is unique, and no single "correct" leader type exists. But by understanding your type, you can identify your strengths and weaknesses and develop strategies for leading more effectively.

Leader Type is also vital because of diversity's role in effective leadership. You can't be as effective if you have a team full of only Enneagram Type Ones. Teams with diverse perspectives and leadership styles are often more resilient and adaptable than teams with singular approaches. By cultivating more diverse and inclusive teams, your organization can better adapt to changing circumstances and be more innovative.

Leadership is a journey, not a destination. Effective leaders constantly learn and grow and are willing to adjust their approach as circumstances change. Different situations and teams may require different approaches to achieve their goals. As a leader, you may need to adapt your approach to be more effective. In order to adapt, you'll need to embrace self-reflection and seek feedback from others to continually improve your leadership skills and positively impact your teams and organizations.

How to Use Leader Type to Become a More Effective Leader

Once you better understand your leader type, you can identify your strengths and weaknesses and develop strategies for leveraging and addressing them. A naturally outgoing and charismatic leader may use these traits to build strong relationships with team members and inspire them to achieve their goals. However, that same person may need help with organization and planning.

With leader type identified, you'll learn to adapt your leadership approach to various follower, team, and stakeholder needs. Team members may respond differently to each leadership type, and someone who knows their leader type can adjust their approach to best meet the team's needs.

ALL ABOUT
AI

Using AI with Your Leader Type to Become an Even More Effective Leader

Once you understand your leader type, you can use AI to identify your strengths and weaknesses more quickly and accurately; it can also provide near-real-time feedback and insights to help you improve your performance and that of your team.

Here are six sometimes surprising ways AI applications can work with your leader type to enhance your effectiveness:

1. **Personality Profiling:** AI-powered tools can administer assessments to team members and generate comprehensive profiles. By understanding the individual personalities of your followers, you gain insights into their strengths, communication styles, motivations, and preferred work environments. This knowledge helps you tailor your leadership approach, assign tasks more effectively, and foster better collaboration.

2. **Team Composition and Dynamics:** AI can analyze the personalities of your team members, providing insights into team composition and dynamics. By examining the compatibility and diversity within the team, AI can suggest strategies to enhance team performance, identify potential areas of conflict, or recommend ways to balance strengths and weaknesses.

3. **Communication Style Analysis:** Special AI systems will analyze communication patterns and provide feedback on individual communication styles. They detect nuances in language, identify potential misunderstandings, and suggest ways to adapt your communication style to different individuals. You'll convey your message more effectively and build rapport with team members.

4. **Conflict Resolution:** AI assists in conflict resolution by analyzing the individuals involved, identifying common sources of conflict, and suggesting effective resolution strategies. By considering the preferences, communication styles, and motivations of each person involved, AI provides guidance on managing each conflict and finding common ground.

5. **Coaching and Development:** AI-powered coaching platforms provide personalized guidance to team members. These tailored recommendations are for professional development, leadership skills, and team building activities. In this case, AI is helping you support the growth and development of your team members in a more targeted and effective manner.

6. **Decision-Making:** AI can provide data-driven insights to support your decision-making process as a leader. AI algorithms can analyze your followers' strengths, expertise, and potential biases to offer recommendations for task assignments, promotions, and team restructuring.

However, it is essential to note that using AI in leadership does not replace human interaction, nor should it make final decisions. While AI can provide valuable insights and support, it is ultimately up to you, the human leader, to make that final decision and take responsibility for the outcome.

REFLECTION QUESTIONS

- Using the Enneagram numbering system, where would you place yourself?

- Does this type of information help increase your level of awareness regarding your habitual patterns, strengths, and growth opportunities?

- How can you use this type-based information to guide how you interact with others to improve your ability to lead and motivate followers?

- Would an increased use of type knowledge help improve your team's effectiveness by promoting discussion among team members about preferred roles and communication styles?

- As we implement AI and other technology systems, how will your understanding of your type and your followers' types help you communicate and interact with them more effectively?

- How will your understanding of your followers' types help you build trust and create psychological safety with individuals and across groups?

DIVE DEEPER

Books

Deep Coaching: Using the Enneagram as a Catalyst for Profound Change by Roxanne Howe-Murphy

Deep Living: Transforming Your Relationship to Everything That Matters Through the Enneagram by Roxanne Howe-Murphy

The Wisdom of the Enneagram: The Complete Guide to Psychological and Spiritual Growth for the Nine Personality Types by Don Richard Riso and Russ Hudson

Underneath Your Personality: Discover Greater Well-Being Through Deep Living with the Enneagram by Roxanne Howe-Murphy

Podcast Episodes

Innovating Leadership: Co-Creating Our Future
Season 3 Episode 17: "Building Leadership Self-Awareness Using Type"

Innovating Leadership: Co-Creating Our Future
Season 4 Episode 20: "Using Enneagram Assessment to Build Leadership Effectiveness"

CHAPTER 4

Developmental Perspectives

Your developmental perspective guides how you see the world and what you do.

CHAPTER 4

Developmental Perspectives

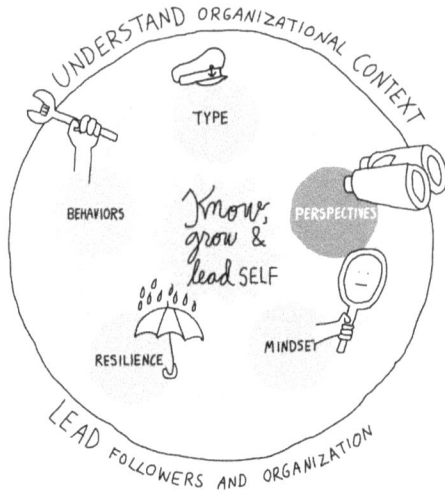

> ***"Yesterday I was clever,
> so I wanted to change the
> world. Today I am wise, so
> I am changing myself."***

Jalal al-Din Rumi wrote those words 800 years ago, and they remain true today. An Innovative Leader continually learns, adapts, grows, and *develops*. Your developmental *perspectives* adapt and grow with you. The world you see around you now looks very different than when you were a toddler — and different from just a few years earlier in your career!

Therefore, it makes perfect sense that these developmental perspectives will influence your relationships with other people: team members, peers, supervisors, clients, and the like. And relationships are key to leading.

What Are Developmental Perspectives?

Developmental Perspectives are the ways we sense and interpret the world around us; think of them as your worldview. We develop both horizontally and vertically. Horizontal development means increasing your general knowledge and abilities. Vertical development refers to increasing understanding of complexity, improving emotional maturity, and expanding openness to new ideas and approaches.

A plethora of elements shape your perspectives: culture, education, family upbringing, mentors, traumas, personal experiences, even a book or movie that resonates with you. Any of these can push you from horizontal development to vertical development.

The good news: you don't have to wait for "life to happen" to grow. You can accelerate your vertical development through intentional actions, specific practices, training, reflection exercises, stretch assignments, exploring cultures, feedback, and coaching from leaders with advanced perspectives. Some organizations are designed to promote vertical development; they are referred to as deliberately developmental organizations (DDO).

Development doesn't happen overnight. It takes years because changing how you interpret and react to the world takes a significant shift in your meaning-making algorithm. Typically, when leaders focus on their development, they take two to five years to shift levels.

In our complex work lives, endless distractions vie for our attention. Holding close to a robust model for personal development helps us focus our energy on our growth. That framework also provides a common language and, most importantly, allows leaders to map where they are now with where they need or want to be to accomplish their goals.

Leader Type & Developmental Perspectives

While leader type is generally constant, you can grow and evolve your developmental perspective. Indeed, great leaders continue to develop over time. Your developmental perspective can become a valuable differentiator in leadership effectiveness.

This model helps us clarify how leaders develop individually and applies to the organizational level to help select and train leaders more effectively.

The Leadership Maturity Model and Developmental Levels/Perspectives

Developmental perspectives models indicate that, over time, people tend to grow and progress through several distinct stages of awareness and ability. One of the most well-known developmental models is Abraham Maslow's

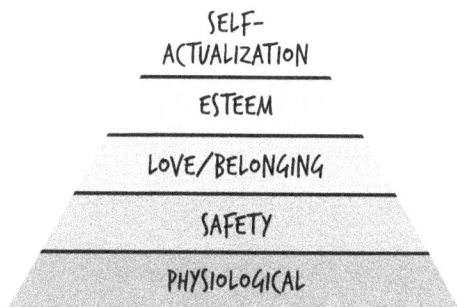

Fig. 4.1: Maslow's Hierarchy of Needs

Hierarchy of Needs — a concept explaining the levels of human needs, both psychological and physical. As you ascend the steps of the pyramid, you can eventually reach self-actualization. Self-actualization represents the pursuit of personal growth, self-fulfillment, and realizing your full potential.

The Developmental Perspective Levels

You're no doubt eager to figure out your current level and the potential levels awaiting you. We'll start with a level people commonly hit in their teens or early adulthood. We're using the descriptive names of the Leadership Maturity Framework (LMF), numbers from the STAGES Model, and names used in the Rooke and Torbert article published by Harvard Business Review.

The Group-Centric Level (2.5, Diplomat)

This level is about *conforming* and *belonging*. People at this level follow the rules and norms and observe hierarchy. They conform to social expectations, work to group standards, seek membership and approval, and appreciate outward signs of status as a sign of approval. They attend to the welfare of their group; those who are not like them are the "other" and, therefore, outside their circle of concern. They avoid conflict. Group-Centric people think and often speak in generalities. Feedback is taken as disapproval because their driving value is to gain approval and be included.

Example: Think of a typical teen coming-of-age movie. In the film *Clueless*, the main characters, Cher and Tai, focus on their peer group. They look at the group's actions to determine their actions. They try to meet the "expectations" set by the organizations in their lives (peers, parents, and school), fit into the culture, and do what everyone does. Belonging is the key to success; standing out or having a different opinion feels risky.

The Skill-Centric Level (3.0, Expert)

This level focuses on *comparing self to others* and *perfecting skills*. Individuals at this level focus on competence in their area of interest and improving techniques and efficiency. They aspire to quality standards and are often heavily invested in their way as the *only* way. Decisions are made based on incontrovertible "facts." Given their focus on problem-solving and detail, they can get caught in the weeds and not see the big picture necessary to prioritize among competing demands effectively. All-consuming attention on being right can make them critical of and competitive with others. They hear feedback about their work as criticism of them as a whole person.

Example: Remember Dwight Schrute from *The Office*? He's very much Skill-Centric: he points out when others make mistakes and tries to correct them so they can meet his standards. A Skill-Centric's development efforts focus on building expertise. As a result, they usually have a "better" opinion unless they are in the presence of a subject-matter expert.

The Self-Determining Level (3.5, Achiever)

This level focuses on *analyzing* and *achieving* to deliver results effectively. Individuals at this level look toward longer-term goals and initiate rather than follow expectations. They value objectivity and scientific knowledge, seeking rational, proactive ways around problems. They often seek consensus — "agree to disagree" — and value mutuality and equality in relationships. Finally, they accept feedback to promote learning and success.

Example: Clark Kent/Superman personifies the Self-Determining level well. He's an achiever who continually drives to meet organizational goals. He works efficiently and effectively and continuously competes with himself and others to drive the best results. He also makes long-term plans, is open to new learning, and becomes more reflective.

The Self-Questioning Level (4.0, Individualist)

This level focuses on the *self in relationship* and *contextualizing* their experience. Individuals at this level are concerned with the difference between reality and appearance and have an increased understanding of the complexity and unintended effects of actions. They question their assumptions and views, realize the subjectivity of beliefs, and talk of interpretations rather than facts. They can play different roles in different contexts and begin to seek out and value feedback.

Example: Compared to Clark Kent/Superman, Diana Prince/Wonder Woman takes development to a new level. As a Self-Questioner, she is constantly inquiring, challenging assumptions, and staying aware of the limitations of conventional thinking. She focuses on creating an environment where everyone feels valued. She is committed to appreciating value from different perspectives.

The Self-Actualizing Level (4.5 Strategist)

This level is about *integrating* and *transforming* self and systems and recognizing higher principles, complexity, and interrelationships. Individuals at this level are aware of the social construction of reality — not just rules and customs. They are problem-finding, not just doing creative problem-solving. They are aware of paradoxes and contradictions in self and systems and learn to appreciate others deeply. They demonstrate a sensitivity to systemic change and create positive-sum games.

Example: Oprah Winfrey is an example of someone who grew to her self-actualizing level. The alternative term "strategist" fits her perfectly: she continually evaluates her personal and company strategies against long-term industry trends, cultural changes, and global economic conditions while embodying her values and using herself as an instrument of transformation. She is self-aware and firmly anchored in her principles while maintaining the ability to adapt based on context.

The Importance of Developmental Perspective

Developmental perspectives significantly influence how you see your role and function in the workplace, interact with others, and solve problems. This is important because the algorithm you use to make sense of the world influences your thoughts and actions.

Some specific benefits of focusing and reflecting on where you are within the levels include having knowledge that can:

- guide you in determining your personal development goals and action plans by helping to understand the next step in either enhancing your abilities at the current perspective or growing into the next perspective;

- help you build a communication strategy and approach to stakeholder groups and departments as well as individual stakeholders and followers;

- help you understand your followers' perspectives and craft solutions that meet the needs of all stakeholders;

- help identify which successors to groom for growth opportunities;

- be used as a tool when determining which individuals and team members best fit specific roles by considering their skills and developmental perspective; and

- help you create interview questions in the hiring process to illuminate key behaviors required for success in the job.

The Developmental Perspectives model can inform your leadership development journey and help you better understand the followers you lead. When you understand how someone perceives the world, you can communicate with them more effectively, motivate them, and provide guidance that aligns with their values and beliefs. This understanding also helps you identify their strengths and weaknesses, so you can assign tasks accordingly and build a more effective team in the process.

Neither you nor your team members are stuck in one stage forever. People can move between stages — forward and backward, depending on their life conditions — throughout their lives. These stages are neither hierarchical nor judgmental. Each stage simply represents a different way of perceiving and interacting with the world, so every stage has its strengths and limitations. By understanding the characteristics associated with each level, you can better understand the needs and perspectives of your team members and tailor your approach to support their growth and development.

Critical Facets of the Developmental Perspectives

When using Developmental Perspective frameworks, please remember:

- ↪ Development does not mean that more developed people are "better" people; organizations can use the vertical development framework as an additional tool to help match people to job roles, in addition to considering their experience and skills. Developmental perspective is a mechanism to evaluate fit for a role along with skill fit and cultural fit. People who test at the later stages will likely be mature enough to be effective in key leadership roles within large, complex organizations.

- ↪ People evolve through levels. There is no skipping of levels, though people do move through the different levels at varying paces.

- ↪ Several organizations offer credible developmental assessments. Individual scores generally range across three to five levels — not just one level. The score reflects an individual's center of gravity, leading edge, and lagging edge. This range reflects healthy development.

- ↪ Keep ethics in mind. This is just one factor, one data point, in painting a picture of a whole person. It's not a judgment but a tool to use alongside a suite of others to assess yourself and your followers, finding not just ideal roles now, but knowing how to guide future growth and development. Weigh developmental perspective along with work history, job performance, personality assessments, and other important elements. Of course, be respectful of privacy and confidentiality; many people feel these assessments are deeply personal.

Applications for Leaders

There are many ways to use knowledge of developmental perspectives to lead and follow more effectively. Here are some specific applications:

1. **Tailor communication style:** Different stages of developmental perspectives may require different communication styles. For example, individuals at the diplomat stage may need specific instructions, while someone at the strategist stage may require more open-ended, creative approaches, and latitude to design their own approach. Tailoring your communication style to match the developmental perspective of your team members builds better relationships and achieves better results.

2. **Improve decision-making and problem-solving:** Understanding developmental perspectives can help you improve decision-making and problem-solving. By recognizing that your team members approach these activities from different perspectives, you can bring together diverse perspectives to create more robust and practical solutions. This understanding can lead to better outcomes for the organization as a whole, too.

3. **Encourage diversity and inclusion:** Knowing developmental perspectives can help create more diverse and inclusive teams. By embracing people's different perspectives on the world, you can create a culture that values and respects different ways of thinking and being. This helps create a more welcoming and supportive work environment for all team members.

4. **Foster team member growth and development:** You can use knowledge of developmental perspectives to foster personal growth and development among your team members.

5. **Identify strengths and growth opportunities:** Understanding team members' stages helps you identify their strengths and weaknesses relative to the tasks they are trying to accomplish (fit-for-role). For example, someone at the diplomat stage may be highly skilled at following rules and norms. In contrast, someone at the individualist stage may be highly creative and innovative. By identifying these strengths and weaknesses, you can assign tasks and responsibilities that play to your team members' strengths, increasing productivity and overall team success. Where team members have growth opportunities, they can work with you to create development plans.

6. **Support growth and development:** Recognizing someone's development stage gives you the insights to provide guidance, coaching, mentoring, training, and other support tailored to team members' needs at different levels.

7. **Build leadership capacity:** The developmental models offer a strong tool to enhance your own self-awareness. You can assess your current level of maturity and where you need to be to best accomplish your professional goals. From there, you can engage in your own development process.

8. **Determine fit-for-role:** Certain developmental levels are ideal for particular roles. A visionary big-picture strategist may not be the best choice for repetitive, highly-detailed microscopic widget assembly! As mentioned in the "Facets" section above, remember to consider multiple factors in addition to a person's developmental stage.

Understanding developmental perspectives is critical to improving individual, team, and organizational effectiveness and impact. Knowing how people perceive and make sense of the world, you can tailor your communication style, identify strengths and weaknesses, foster personal growth and development, encourage diversity and inclusion, and improve decision-making and problem-solving.

As artificial intelligence evolves, you'll also be able to use AI-powered assessments, personalized development plans, coaching, augmented reality training, and natural language processing. This gives you targeted feedback and support tailored to your specific needs and stage of development.

On the human side, you'll also feel more personally fulfilled as a leader; effectively using these developmental models boosts your ability to inspire, motivate, and support your team.

How Can AI Facilitate Vertical Development?

ALL ABOUT

AI

AI can be a powerful tool for helping you (and your followers) grow through developmental perspective levels. Here are some specific ways:

1. **AI-Based Assessments:** AI can develop the assessments that help you better understand your current stage of ego development, as well as the development of your team.

2. **Personalized Development Plans:** Based on the results of these assessments, AI could then create personalized development plans tailored to a person's specific stage of development.

3. **Coaching to Augment Human Coaches:** AI can guide you as you work through your development plan. This coaching can take the most convenient form for you, such as chatbots or virtual assistants that provide real-time feedback and support tailored to your needs.

4. **Augmented Reality Training:** This type of training uses AI to create realistic simulations of complex scenarios you might face in your work. Simulations can be customized to your specific stage of development and provide a safe space for you to practice new skills and behaviors.

5. **Natural Language Processing:** AI can analyze the language you use in your communications. This provides insights into your level of cognitive complexity, emotional intelligence, and ability to handle complexity and ambiguity. Then you receive targeted feedback and support while you develop your leadership skills.

REFLECTION QUESTIONS

- As you read about developmental perspectives, which levels resonate most for you?

- Think about your next promotion: what developmental perspective level will be required for you to perform effectively in that role?

- Are you a good developmental fit for your current role? If not, should you be in a more senior role or a more junior role?

- As you review the levels, how might you shift your communication style to work more effectively with followers, colleagues, and partners who operate at different developmental perspectives?

- Does your developmental perspective range support you in leading complex technology and AI changes?

- Have you seen one or two things people at later perspectives do differently than you do? What steps can you take to close this gap?

DIVE DEEPER

Articles

"Seven Transformations of Leadership" by David Rooke and William R. Torbert (Harvard Business Review)

"What Is the Path for Leadership Maturity?" by Maureen Metcalf (Forbes Coaches Council)

Podcast Episodes

Innovating Leadership: Co-Creating Our Future
Season 4 Episode 14: "Organizational Development: Understanding Human Development"

Innovating Leadership: Co-Creating Our Future
Season 4 Episode 38: "How Developmental Maturity Aligns with Organizational Maturity"

Note: There are several different models explaining developmental perspectives. We reference vertical development models grounded in research by Robert Kegan, Susanne Cook-Greuter, David Rooke, William R. Torbert, and Terri O'Fallon.

Other developmental perspective models include: Ego Development Model, STAGES Model, Action Logics, and Constructive Developmental Theory (stages of adult development). The labels we use integrate those models' names and numbers in parentheses, so if you are more familiar with another model, you can cross-reference with LMF.

· CHAPTER 5 ·

Mindsets

Your mindset impacts how you see yourself and the world, and is a foundation for your behavior.

CHAPTER 5

Mindset

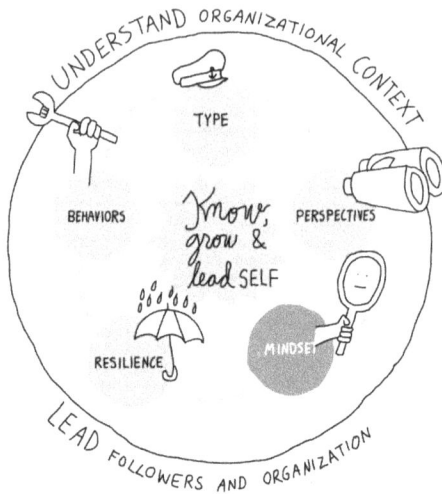

The magician and illusionist Harry Houdini performed amazing feats that seem impossible to this day. But there's a very simple secret to his success: mindsets.

A mindset is a set of beliefs, attitudes, and assumptions creating the mental framework that guides your thoughts and actions.

Magicians and illusionists employ their own mindsets of discipline and achievement to stay underwater in chains for minutes at a time and perform other astonishing acts of endurance. And they exploit our mindsets to believe their impossible illusions are real.

Your use of mindsets is no less important. Leadership is more than having a title or position. It is about having a mindset that enables you to inspire, guide, and support yourself and others to achieve common goals. Now, more than ever before, we need to adapt to new ways of working on and leading our teams. To succeed, we need to develop new mindsets that enable us to navigate the complexities of our changing workplaces.

In this chapter, we discuss the mindset that underpins your actions. Moving an organization forward only happens when leaders are able to inspire followers to follow them. Mindsets are relevant to making this happen.

What Are Leadership Mindsets?

We identified seven mindsets that influence your effectiveness as a leader. This Innovative Leadership Institute Leadership Mindsets Model draws on the developmental model you read about in the previous chapter (Developmental Perspectives). Specifically, our mindsets model aligns with the strategist's developmental perspective. Each mindset holds a corresponding set of behaviors. All seven are measurable and can be effectively used to facilitate your developmental growth.

Remember, a mindset informs how you make sense of the world. And the way you see the world drives how you behave. While few people operate entirely from the strategist perspective, adopting their characteristic behaviors is a way to work toward that level. It also provides insights into what highly mature leaders generally experience while working at their highest potential.

The table below details the seven mindsets and their associated leadership behaviors.

TABLE 5.1: ILI (INNOVATIVE LEADERSHIP INSTITUTE) LEADERSHIP MINDSETS MODEL™	
Professionally Humble	*Cares more about the organization's success than their own success and image*
	⤳ Committed to their personal and organizational mission as a "north star." It's a focal point for where to invest their energy in service of making a positive impact and leaving a legacy.
	⤳ Cares more about the team, organization, and results than their personal image.
	⤳ Gives credit to others.
	⤳ Puts individual and organizational principles ahead of personal gain.
Unwavering Commitment to the Right Action	*Is unstoppable and unflappable when on a mission*
	⤳ Commits fully, drives hard, and focuses, but is not overly focused or stubborn.
	⤳ Stays the course under pressure and also dares to change course when a better approach emerges.

A 360-Degree Thinker	*Takes a systems view — understanding the context and interconnectedness of systems when making critical decisions*
	↩ Understands the systems, constraints, and perceptions, as well as the near-term, long-term, and secondary impacts of strategy and decisions; also understands how to transform them to deliver meaningful results.
	↩ Balances competing commitments of multiple stakeholders.
	↩ Has a strong commitment to continuous personal learning and building systems within the organization that promote learning.
	↩ Understands cross-organizational impact and interconnections across multiple complex systems. Makes highly informed decisions considering implications across broad contexts.
	↩ Thinks in terms of systems, constraints, and perceptions when focusing on transformation. Considers context as a foundation for critical decisions.
Intellectually Versatile	*Develops interests, expertise, and curiosity beyond the job and organization: life-long learner*
	↩ Despite a devout commitment to the job and the organization, is always interested and involved with areas beyond their comfort zone.
	↩ Takes particular interest in their ecosystem, including industry-wide activities, political developments, and the international landscape.
	↩ Uses external interests to make an impact, enhance their legacy and provide balance in life.
Highly Authentic and Reflective	*Not constrained by personal image but highly focused on individual behavior*
	↩ Highly committed to personal growth and development, and growing and developing others.
	↩ Extremely open to feedback and non-defensive.
	↩ Seeks out discussions and feedback even in uncomfortable situations.
	↩ Manages emotions in the most challenging situations. Understands the impact and contagious nature of emotions, develops skills to recognize and manage them, and relate to others productively.
	↩ Maintains perspective in times of stress, taking a long-term view and remaining vision focused. Difficult situations challenge them less than others.
	↩ Demonstrates emotional courage — willing to confront challenging situations.
	↩ Continually looks for ways to enable the team and organization to improve its ability to meet its mission more efficiently and effectively.

Inspires Followership	*Has a remarkable ability to connect with people at all levels of the organization to create a shared vision*
	→ Understands that change is necessary to sustain the team and organization's ability to meet its mission. Knows the steps to managing change and helping the organization overcome its resistance.
	→ Diffuses conflict without avoiding or sidestepping the source of the conflict.
	→ Uses humor effectively to put people at ease.
	→ Relates to a broad range of people and understands their motivators and stressors.
	→ Connects projects to individual goals while working to overcome barriers.
	→ Provides valuable feedback to others in a manner that is supportive of the recipient's growth and development.
Innately Collaborative	*Welcomes collaboration in a quest for novel solutions that serve the highest outcome for all involved*
	→ Seeks input and values diverse points of view. Synthesizes multiple perspectives into new solutions.
	→ Creates solutions to complex problems by developing new approaches that did not exist, pulling together constituents in novel ways, and synthesizing broader and more creative alliances.
	→ Understands that in times of extreme change, input from multiple stakeholders with diverse viewpoints is required to fully understand the complexities of the issues.

Why Are Leadership Mindsets Important?

First, Leadership Mindsets enable you to navigate complex and uncertain environments. In today's world, change is constant, so you need to adapt quickly to new circumstances. Mindsets such as *humility* and *commitment to right action* enable you to do this effectively.

Second, Leadership Mindsets enable you to connect with and inspire your team. Inspiring followership, as well as authentic and reflective behaviors, are essential to building strong relationships and creating a culture of trust and respect. When team members feel valued and heard, they are more likely to be engaged and committed to the organization's goals.

Third, these mindsets enable you to drive innovation and growth. For example, the *intellectually versatile* and *innately collaborative* mindsets are necessary to create a culture of continuous learning and improvement. Leaders who embrace an *intellectually versatile* mindset are more likely to enable their teams to take risks and experiment with new ideas (in other words, to be innovative!).

Developing Leadership Mindsets

We don't want to mislead you: developing Leadership Mindsets is not easy. Changing an underlying belief is different from building a skill. You spent a lifetime shaping the way you see the world; that won't shift overnight. Here are some strategies that can help you develop those seven essential Leadership Mindsets:

1. **Learn from others:** seek mentors and role models who embody the mindsets you want to develop. Observe how they approach challenges and interact with others. Ask them to explain their thoughts and why they made their choices. Try to identify the internal beliefs and attitudes that drove their behavior. What did they see? Why did they act as they acted? Don't be shy about this; most people are happy to share their wisdom and experiences.

2. **Practice self-reflection:** examine your thoughts, beliefs, assumptions, and behaviors. Ask yourself whether they are serving you well or holding you back. Challenge yourself to adopt new perspectives and ways of thinking.

3. **Seek feedback:** ask your team members, peers, and superiors for honest feedback. Encourage them to inform you when you demonstrate behaviors associated with the mindsets, and when you don't. Stop and reflect immediately — ask what you thought, felt, or believed that enabled you (or, on the flip side, that challenged you). You can shift your beliefs by building on your positive beliefs and feelings and learning where your negative beliefs are a barrier.

4. **Educate yourself:** read books and articles, listen to podcasts, and engage with other resources focusing on leadership development and the mindsets you want to develop. Attend workshops and conferences that focus on developing Leadership Mindsets. Participate in a leadership development course, or hire a coach for more personalized one-on-one learning.

5. **Create a learning culture:** as a leader, you can create a culture of learning within your team and organization. Encourage your team members to explore their own mindsets and the results they produce. When we examine the impact of our mindsets, we can become aware of suboptimal impacts and reinforce the new mindsets — celebrating mindset and corresponding outcome successes and failures are opportunities for growth and learning.

6. **Embrace discomfort:** developing new mindsets can be uncomfortable and challenging. Embrace this discomfort and use it as an opportunity to learn and grow.

7. **Practice mindfulness:** take time daily to practice mindfulness exercises such as deep breathing, meditation, or yoga. These exercises can help you develop greater self-awareness and empathy for others, as well as the ability to reflect in the moment, supporting evolving mindsets. BONUS: An abundance of medical research shows physical benefits to mindfulness practices, too.

8. **Foster diversity and inclusion:** develop an inclusive mindset by actively seeking out and valuing diverse perspectives among your team members. Encourage open communication and collaboration among team members from diverse backgrounds and those with different and innovative ways of thinking.

9. **Engage a leadership coach:** this person can help you understand your developmental journey by helping you reflect on your progress as well as planning your development as a leader. This person can help you recognize your — and your team's — potential.

10. **Take assessments:** to better understand your strengths and opportunities, take coach-administered assessments to help identify your leadership mindset and developmental perspective.

To summarize: developing Leadership Mindsets is essential for success in today's fast-paced and ever-changing world. Mindsets such as *humility, 360-degree thinking, intellectual curiosity*, and *innate collaboration* enable you to navigate complexity, connect with and inspire your team, and drive innovation and growth. Developing these mindsets requires self-reflection, feedback, learning from others, and embracing discomfort. As a leader, you can create a culture of learning and inclusion within your organization by developing these mindsets. You can inspire, guide, and support yourself and your team to be future-ready leaders and create a future-ready organization.

Developing Mindsets Using AI

AI can help you develop the leadership mindsets you need to thrive in our fast-paced and ever-changing world. Here are some ways to use it:

1. **Identify Areas for Improvement:** As with your vertical development, AI-powered assessment tools can help identify your strengths and weaknesses as a leader. An added benefit to AI assessments is that these tools can analyze data from various sources, such as performance metrics and personality assessments, generating personalized feedback and guidance on improving your leadership skills.

2. **Recommend Learning Tools:** AI-powered learning platforms adjust your learning experience based on your needs and preferences. Like the assessments above, these use data from various sources, including job performance metrics, to identify learning opportunities and suggest relevant content.

3. **Inspire Followership:** AI's sentiment analysis tools help you understand your team's emotions and perspectives. These tools analyze data from various sources, such as chat logs and social media activity, to identify trends and patterns in your team members' feelings. This can help you develop greater empathy and build stronger relationships with your team.

4. **Develop 360-Degree Thinking:** AI excels at predictive analytics and idea generation; these tools identify information from a range of sources, help you understand interconnected systems, and anticipate and prepare for future challenges by analyzing past data to identify patterns and trends. This is a great boon in making data-driven decisions and developing proactive strategies to address potential risks and opportunities.

REFLECTION QUESTIONS

- Do you focus on achieving the best outcome for your organization above being right or perfect?

- Are you fully committed to doing the work to accomplish challenging goals?

- Are you willing to adjust direction based on new information?

- Are you curious and committed to staying informed on a wide range of topics that directly and indirectly impact your organization?

- Do you continue to innovate your thinking and behavior and help others grow and develop while building a culture of learning and innovation in your organization?

- Do you build trust by communicating openly, honestly, and empathetically understanding the challenges your team faces during change?

- Do you encourage others to share their candid input?

DIVE DEEPER

Articles

"Leading Post-Pandemic and Beyond: Innovative Leadership" by Erin Barry, Neil Grunberg, Maureen Metcalf, Carla Morelli, and Michael Morrow-Fox (Cutter)

"Seven Key Crisis Leadership Skills" by Maureen Metcalf (Forbes Coaches Council)

Blog Posts

Innovative Leadership Institute Insights Blog October 15, 2015 Post: "Leadership 2050 Competency Model"

Innovative Leadership Institute Insights Blog October 11, 2021 Post: "Are You a Future-Ready Leader?"

Books

Reinventing Organizations: A Guide to Creating Organizations Inspired by the Next Stage of Human Consciousness by Frederic Laloux

Podcast Episodes

Innovating Leadership: Co-Creating Our Future
Season 1 Episode 14: "What Does the Leader of the Future Really Look Like?"

Innovating Leadership: Co-Creating Our Future
Season 7 Episode 29: "The New Role of Leadership in a Hybrid Workplace"

· CHAPTER 6 ·

Resilience

As leaders, we need to surf the waves of change and have enough energy left to lead our followers.

CHAPTER 6

Resilience

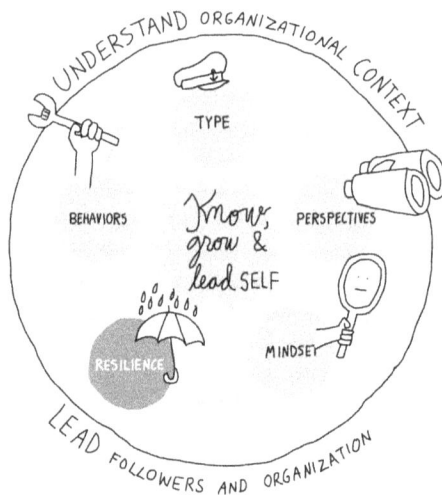

From Gloria Gaynor's iconic "I Will Survive" to Kelly Clarkson's "What Doesn't Kill You Makes You Stronger," many artists have sung about getting up again after a fall. Giants in history — Helen Keller, Mahatma Gandhi, Martin Luther King, Jr., and most recently, Greta Thunberg — have embodied this will to bounce back from difficult, even dire, obstacles and challenges.

It's called resilience, and it's a mental superpower that gives you the ability to rebound from setbacks, adapt to change, and thrive during and after adversity. This chapter explains resilience, why it's essential, and how to develop it as a leader.

What Is Resilience?

Resilience: Noun. The capacity to adapt to challenges and difficulties; mental flexibility in the face of obstacles or external demands.

That's the technical definition. In practice, there's more nuance to resilience for a leader. First, its strength depends greatly on your physical, psychological, and social well-being. Second, resilience can be amplified by *antifragility*, a relatively new term that means not only bouncing back from challenges but improving because of them. And third, you must also be adaptable in your leadership approach and remain focused on your strategic goals (although *how* you attain them is flexible).

Addressing all aspects of resilience is critical to managing stress and increasing your baseline capacity to function in stressful environments. The ultimate goal of resilience is to "thrive" — that is, to become stronger after facing adversity and challenges.

Resilience can be developed and strengthened over time. As a leader, facing challenges and obstacles is inevitable. Your ability to bounce back is critical to success.

FROM OUR FILES: DO THE IMPOSSIBLE

The CIO of a major state university asked Maureen about the tension between support and challenge. How much support should they give to enable people to grow, and how do they balance that with the inevitable challenges of the job?

The CIO's instinct was simple: let the team *learn* to do hard things by *doing* hard things.

It rang true to Maureen. Every successful leader Maureen has worked with accomplished something they never imagined possible. Sure, they made mistakes and felt embarrassed by how they faced the challenges. Yet, one consistent outcome emerged with every single leader: they built enough resilience to move forward.

Such leaders send a strong message to their followers by modeling resilience. And because of their own stumbles and embarrassments, these effective leaders create a psychologically safe environment. We're more able to do hard things when we trust our leaders to support us.

Why Is Resilience Important?

Resilience is essential for leaders because it helps us navigate difficult situations and overcome challenges. Resilient leaders can maintain their focus and motivation amid setbacks and adversity. They're also better equipped to adapt to change — an ever-present constant in today's work environment.

Among the elements essential to leadership, Resilience is unique; it integrates both the physical and psychological aspects of Leader Type, Developmental

Perspectives, and Mindset, creating the foundation of a leader's inner stability. This foundation enables you to demonstrate fluidity and endurance as you adapt to ongoing change. There's a wonderful side effect, too: your resilience is contagious; it infects the people around you, positively impacting others.

Resilience also builds trust and credibility with your team. Demonstrating it shows your team you can handle challenges and setbacks, which inspires confidence in your leadership. Resilient leaders set an example for their team, showing them how to bounce back from whatever difficulties cross their path.

Underlying Resilience is the necessity to be physically and emotionally healthy in order to do an excellent job as a leader. In addition to physical and emotional health, the resilient leader has a clear sense of life purpose, exceptional emotional intelligence, and strong supportive relationships. Those are deeply personal traits; as a result, for most people, enhancing Resilience requires personal change.

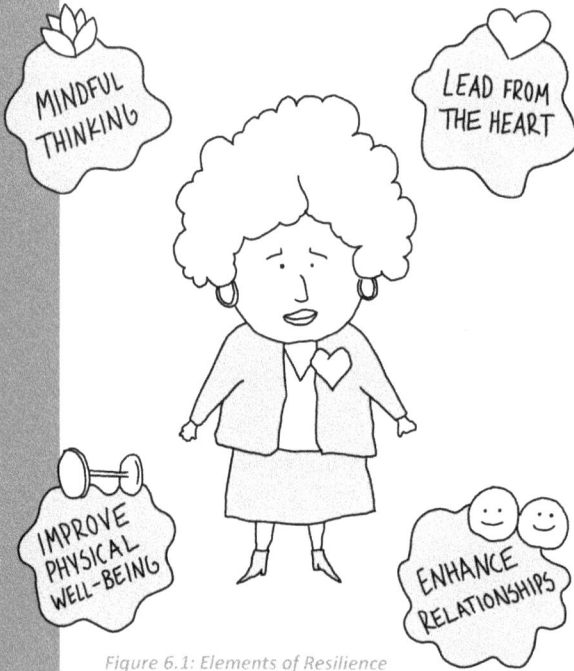

Figure 6.1: Elements of Resilience

Our Resilience model has four categories:

- Improve Physical Well-Being
- Mindful Thinking
- Lead from the Heart
- Enhance Relationships

These categories are interlinked and must be balanced to create long-term Resilience.

Leaders we work with often say they are too busy to take care of themselves. Finding the balance between self-care and meeting our daily commitments is challenging! Yet, leaders are their own most essential instruments of leadership, so caring for yourself is crucial. Most people fall short of their fitness and self-care goals and, over the long term, make choices *for* or *against* Resilience and personal health. These choices are sneaky: "I don't have time for lunch today" or "It's easier if I schedule these meetings in place of my morning walk this week." Those little decisions are cumulative; eventually, they take over. Make it a habit to prioritize self-care *daily*.

Contrary to your let's-skip-it-today thoughts, a little downtime to "sharpen your saw" boosts productivity and your leadership influence. Fortunately, as you improve your Resilience, you will think more clearly and have a more significant and positive impact on your interactions with others. Investing in Resilience supports the entire organization's effectiveness.

How to Build Resilience

The following table has a few suggestions for building resilience.

TABLE 6.1: KEYS TO BUILDING & RETAINING PERSONAL RESILIENCE

Improve Physical Well-Being	Lead from the Heart

Are you getting enough
 	
  ⤳ Sleep
  ⤳ Exercise
  ⤳ Healthy food
  ⤳ Time in nature
  ⤳ Time to meditate & relax
 	
Are you limiting or eliminating
 	
  ⤳ Caffeine
  ⤳ Nicotine
	Understand what you stand for, and maintain focus. Ask:
	
	  ⤳ What is my purpose?
	  ⤳ Am I actively living my life in alignment with my purpose?
	  ⤳ What values do I hold? How do I live these values in my work and life?
	  ⤳ Do I have a practice that allows me to connect with my feelings and share them with others?
	  ⤳ How do I show compassion for my colleagues?
	  ⤳ Do I find opportunities to make a positive and uplifting impact in all of my interactions?

Mindful Thinking	Enhance Relationships
Practice telling yourself:	Practice effective communication:
↪ Challenges are normal and healthy for any individual or organization. ↪ My current problem is a doorway to an innovative solution. ↪ I feel inspired by the opportunity to create new possibilities that did not exist before.	↪ Say things simply and clearly. ↪ Communicate with empathy. ↪ Make communication safe by listening, inquiring, and being responsive. ↪ Encourage people to ask questions and clarify if they do not understand your message. ↪ Balance advocacy for your point by inquiring about the other person's perspectives. ↪ When you have a different perspective, seek to understand how and why the other person believes what they do in a non-threatening way. ↪ When in doubt, share information and emotions. ↪ Build trust by acting for the greater good.

Remember that amplified form of resilience we mentioned at the beginning of the chapter? Beyond flexibility and adaptability, being anti-fragile means you can actually grow and thrive in our current environment of volatility, uncertainty, complexity, and ambiguity (VUCA). This applies not only to people, but systems as well. Anti-fragile systems not only survive under stress; they become more robust and adaptable as a result of it. Particularly in light of how exponential the growth and changes of artificial intelligence are hitting our work lives, embracing this mindset — and building anti-fragile systems, teams, organizations, and cultures — is a strategy for both success and career survival.

With VUCA growing exponentially, building resilience in your team is undeniably essential. Your team members **will** face challenges and setbacks, and building resilience will help them navigate through these difficulties. Drawing from the table you just read, here are some ways you can build your team's anti-fragile abilities:

- ↪ **Encourage open communication:** Create a culture of open communication where team members feel comfortable sharing their challenges and setbacks. This culture will help them feel supported and help them work through their difficulties. Neurological studies have shown that the same areas of the brain responsible for the 'fight or flight' response also activate when a person feels rejection. In other words, your brain processes rejection and other unsupportive reactions to ideas the same way it processes the threat of a lion getting ready to pounce on you. As leaders, we need to understand this neurological reaction to create team environments that support positive reinforcement for open communication.

- **Provide resources and support:** Ensure your team members can access the resources and support they need to overcome challenges; this can include training, coaching, HR support, EAP (such as counseling services), and more. Employees — particularly those who know how to enhance their skills with AI and other tech tools — are more empowered than ever to find work that pays fairly and employers who treat them with dignity and respect. Providing resources shows your team members that you care about them as a whole person — not just a generic drone there to work for the organization. Our professional and personal lives overlap immensely, which means that when you struggle in one area, the other area can be affected. Consider what resources you can provide as a leader (and ultimately as an organization) to ensure your team members are mentally and physically healthy. A great starting point is to ask team members about their professional goals and how **you** *can help them attain those goals* — it may surprise you how many team members are positively impacted by this simple question.

- **Celebrate successes:** Celebrating successes, even small ones, helps build a positive team culture and boosts morale. This, in turn, helps team members stay motivated and focused, even during challenging times. When team members know they are appreciated, they are more likely to take their work seriously, even give it a little extra. Tie these celebrations in with the professional goals you asked them about, updates on how success impacts bigger team goals, the growth it spurred in their development, and so on.

- **Foster a sense of purpose:** Help your team members connect with the purpose of their work. Knowing their work is meaningful is yet another way team members are more likely to stay motivated and resilient, even when faced with challenges. More than ever, people long for purposeful employment; this is particularly strong in Millennials and Gen Z. Disillusionment from the COVID pandemic permanently realigned much of our thinking around work and the kind of contributions we each would like to bring to the world. Having a grounded sense of purpose (or mission) helps us realign when facing challenges.

Remember the overarching key point of this chapter: as our world becomes increasingly complex, resilience has become an increasingly important behavior for you to develop. Highly effective leaders pay attention to *who* they are, *how* they relate, and *what* they do. To reach optimal performance, you must manage your resilience and become anti-fragile, responding quickly to setbacks. This helps you navigate through difficult situations and overcome challenges while better equipping you to adapt to change and build trust and credibility with your team. Developing resilience requires time, effort, and commitment, so be patient. You'll become more resilient and effective by prioritizing self-care, shifting thinking, leading from your heart, enhancing relationships, and becoming anti-fragile.

How Can AI Help Leaders Build Resilience?

ALL ABOUT

AI

AI technology helps leaders manage their workload, reduce stress, and make more informed decisions. Here are five more ways AI can help you build resilience:

1. **Scheduling and task management.** Leaders often have a lot on their plate, so managing their workload can be a source of stress. If that's you, let AI schedule and prioritize your tasks, manage your time more effectively, and reduce feeling overwhelmed. These tools can also help you judiciously delegate tasks to team members, reducing your workload and freeing up time for self-care.

2. **Predictive analytics for risk management.** You need to identify and manage risks to avoid potential setbacks and crises. AI-powered predictive analytics tools can help identify potential risks and opportunities. These tools help you make more informed decisions and reduce the impact of potential risks.

3. **Mental health and well-being tools.** All the tools in this list help you manage stress, improve your mood, and build resilience. But some AI tools specifically target your state of mind: meditation and mindfulness apps, mood-tracking tools, and emotional support chatbots.

4. **Decision-making.** As a leader, you'll often need to make informed decisions promptly to avoid potential setbacks, delays, and crises. AI-powered decision-making tools help with that process by analyzing large amounts of data, identifying patterns, and making more informed decisions. You can also automate routine decisions with them, freeing up time for more critical decision-making. This has a cascade effect: seeing you use these tools, your team will feel more comfortable integrating them into their workdays, too.

5. **Feedback and performance evaluation.** AI's feedback and performance evaluation tools give real-time feedback on your leadership style, communication skills, and team dynamics. These tools help you identify areas for improvement, adjust your approach, and build your resilience over time.

It's worth reiterating that AI technology can help with a key to resilience many — if not most — leaders ignore: prioritizing self-care. It's not just the obvious #3 in the list above; the others save you time and energy. These tools are quickly becoming more sophisticated and helpful. However, be discerning and use AI like any other tool, ensuring it can add value to the unique way *you* work.

REFLECTION QUESTIONS

Where would you rank your resilience in each of the four categories?

- How does increased resilience improve your effectiveness as a person and leader?

- What is your biggest resilience challenge?

- Think of areas in your life where you may indulge in negative thinking. What steps can you take to increase your mindfulness and replace negative thinking with positive thinking?

- If you are overly challenged, how can you build resilience skills to reduce your anxiety?

- What are you doing that supports or hinders building and maintaining friendships? What steps could you take to initiate or deepen those connections?

- If you were to make progress on your biggest resilience challenge, what small step could you commit to over the next month that will help you improve your resilience?

DIVE DEEPER

Articles

"Managing with the Brain in Mind" by David Rock (Strategy + business)

Blog Posts

Innovative Leadership Institute Insights Blog August 3rd, 2022 Post: "Innovative Leadership: Moving Beyond Resilience to Antifragility"

Books

The Infinite Game by Simon Sinek

The Social Ecology of Resilience: A Handbook of Theory and Practice by Michael Ungar

Film

It's VUCA: The Secret to Living in the 21st Century directed by Chris Nolan

Podcast Episodes

Innovating Leadership: Co-Creating Our Future
Season 8 Episode 36: "Facing Uncertainty: It's VUCA"

Innovating Leadership: Co-Creating Our Future
Season 3 Episode 32: "Building Resilience: A Key Foundation for Change"

Innovating Leadership: Co-Creating Our Future
Season 4 Episode 36: "How Does the Brain Impact Leadership Resilience?"

Skills and Behaviors

As leaders, we need role-based, industry, and transcendent leadership skills and behaviors.
Weakness in any one area causes us to be a leadership "weakling."

CHAPTER 7

Skills and Behaviors

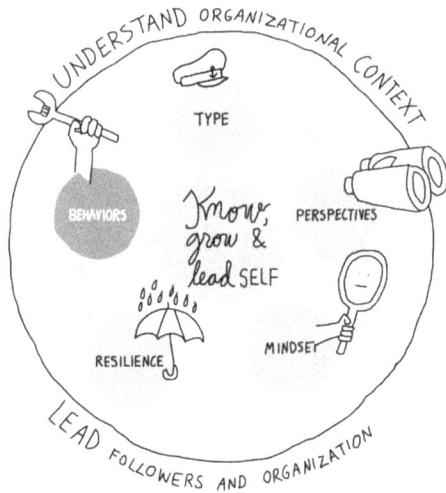

"*Tennis is mostly mental. Of course, you must have a lot of physical skill, but you can't play tennis well and not be a good thinker. You win or lose the match before you even go out there.*"

Venus Williams
(March 2003 in *O, The Oprah Magazine*)

The arena may be different, but in the workplace, as on the tennis court, you're expected to have a particular set of skills and styles of behavior. Those can determine your success "before you even go out there" in a new role. This is all the more true when you're a leader.

Leaders must demonstrate knowledge, skills, and behaviors relevant to their teams and organizations to achieve desired missions and goals. Followers can see your competence through your behaviors and impact on your team members and organization. This element of our framework is observable; while the other aspects are about internal thinking and processes, your skills and actions are visible and used to evaluate your success.

Let's revisit the example of our conductor to help understand the skills and behaviors required for success. The conductor needs *role-specific skills*, including understanding how to play multiple instruments, what music to choose that best fits the musicians' abilities, and the knowledge and behavior to conduct effectively. The conductor must also have *transcendent leadership skills* and *behaviors*, including inspiring the musicians to give their best performances, solving problems or difficulties that may arise during rehearsals and concerts, and providing resources to optimize success.

In other words, leaders need leadership skills and competencies relevant to a particular role, plus broader skills that apply to any role, such as decision-making, problem-solving, emotional intelligence, and conflict resolution.

- **Role-specific skills** include *industry-related knowledge*, such as understanding the hospitality industry's operation, and *functional expertise*, such as hospitality finance or human relations.

- **Transcendent leadership skills** include setting a vision and people-related abilities.

- **Leadership behaviors** refer to the process of putting skills into action, especially transcendent leadership skills. To be competent, leaders need a combination of knowledge, skills, and adaptation to context (situations, personnel, resources) to put into practice, resulting in leadership behaviors.

While role-specific and transcendent leadership skills and behaviors are essential, their value shifts as you progress in your career. Transcendent leadership skills and behaviors become increasingly necessary as you advance to senior levels. We have seen people selected to move into leadership for their industry and role-based skills rather than their leadership behaviors. If they build leadership skills, they will be effective as leaders. We have all seen brilliant people in leadership roles damage their organization because they lacked proper Leadership Behaviors, and we have seen other leaders continually behave well and build ongoing organizational success because they consistently demonstrate Leadership Behaviors.

FROM OUR FILES: THE CEO CHECK-UP

As a hospital CEO, Taylor needs healthcare-specific skills and Leadership Behaviors.

Taylor's professional journey began as a trauma surgeon. Those are powerful but extremely role-specific skills. Leaving the operating theater for the C-suite, Taylor must demonstrate healthcare skills; hospital ops skills to understand how the buildings, departments, and staff function; and Leadership Behaviors to lead people and the organization effectively.

If Taylor lacks these skills, she and the hospital risk damage — even patient lives.

Early in her career, a mastery of surgery set Taylor apart from her peers. As she progressed into senior leadership ranks and into the pinnacle role of CEO, effectively demonstrating Leadership Behaviors became her primary focus and the differentiator in the organization's success. While Taylor never lost the ability to work as a surgeon, she now relies much less on those functional skills and more on leadership skills and behaviors to guide her direction and actions.

Knowing how and when to lean on role-specific and transcendent skills, and the Leadership Behaviors to act on them, makes for a healthy career trajectory.

We use the Leadership Circle Profile (LCP) assessment as an integral part of the ILI model. The whole model is described in *Mastering Leadership: An Integrated Framework for Breakthrough Performance and Extraordinary Business Results.*

The LCP aligns with the Enneagram Leader Type framework, the Developmental Perspectives frameworks, and the leadership mindsets you read about in prior chapters. There are also other valuable models (e.g., Skillscope).

Growing as a leader involves continually modifying your behaviors based on your organizational role, followers' needs, and the industry and organizational context. A clear framework and assessment tool allows you to measure your growth over time.

What Leadership Behaviors Do I Need to Be Successful?

The LCP tracks and measures core behavior patterns, underlying beliefs, established assumptions, and habits of thought. They fall into four broad categories of Leadership Behaviors shown in *Figure 7.1: The Leadership Circle Profile assessment: Relationship, Task, Creative, and Reactive.*

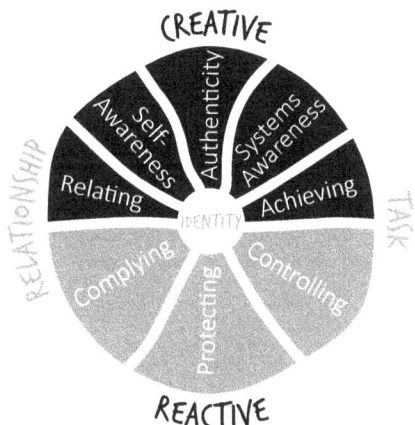

CREATIVE

Self Awareness
Authenticity
Systems Awareness
Relating
Achieving
IDENTITY
Complying
Protecting
Controlling
RELATIONSHIP
TASK

REACTIVE

Figure 7.1: The Leadership Circle Profile assessment:
Relationship, Task, Creative, and Reactive

Behaviors dealing with relationships and tasks are relatively self-explanatory: they are people-oriented or action-oriented, respectively. These distinguish between a leader's role in relating to people versus doing leadership tasks. As a rule of thumb, think about an even split between these two crucial elements. They vary across roles and levels within the organization. In a sense, they're also the borders between strong creative and reactive behaviors.

Creative behaviors focus on growth, development, and progress, while reactive behaviors focus on protection and safety. Let's explore them in more detail.

Creative behaviors include

1. **Relating:** Building robust relationships with your team members based on trust and mutual respect. Leaders who value relationships can create a supportive and collaborative environment.

2. **Self-Awareness:** Understanding your strengths, opportunities, and blind spots. Self-aware leaders can leverage their strengths and address their opportunities for growth to become more effective leaders.

3. **Authenticity:** Being genuine and honest with yourself, your followers, and your team members. Authentic leaders are comfortable with their vulnerabilities and can openly share them.

4. **Systems Awareness:** Understanding the complex systems and processes that drive the organization. Leaders aware of the systems can make more informed decisions that benefit the organization.

5. **Achieving:** Having a clear and inspiring vision of where you want to take your followers, team, and the organization and focusing on setting the strategy, making good decisions, and delivering results required to accomplish the purpose.

Reactive behaviors, on the other hand, include

1. **Controlling:** The tendency to micromanage and focus on details. Reactive leaders often need more trust in their followers and team members and may feel the need to control everything.

2. **Complying:** The tendency to follow the rules and adhere to the status quo. Reactive leaders may resist change and need to adapt to new circumstances.

3. **Protecting:** The tendency to be defensive and avoid taking risks. Reactive leaders may prioritize safety over growth and development.

Being creative gives us more choices in anticipating situations and crafting our responses. When we are reactive, we have fewer options.

Note that all leaders exhibit Creative and Reactive behaviors to some degree. The key is to develop more Creative behaviors while minimizing Reactive behaviors to become a more effective leader. That said, situations — such as a breaking crisis — require leaders to leverage reactive behaviors. The most effective leaders work to lead their organizations from the creative zone but are ready to use reactive behaviors effectively when needed.

Why Are Leadership Behaviors Important?

Leadership Behaviors are essential because they drive impact. Effective leadership behaviors fuel team and organizational success; conversely, ineffective leadership behaviors steer you toward team and organizational dysfunction or failure. You've probably seen (or, sadly, experienced) leaders who leave a trail of destruction in their wake: they consistently behave in a manner that damages their followers, teams, and even the entire organization. That is not the leader you want to imitate (or you wouldn't have picked up this book), so let's examine the behaviors of those *other* leaders — the ones who promote ongoing organizational success.

When successful leaders exhibit Creative behaviors, they inspire and motivate their followers to achieve great things. When leaders exhibit Reactive behaviors as their norm — instead of in exceptional circumstances only — they create a culture of fear and mistrust that holds the organization back.

Creative leadership behaviors can

1. **Build Trust:** When you exhibit authenticity and build strong relationships with your followers, the resulting trust creates a culture of collaboration and innovation.

2. **Drive Innovation:** Expressing a clear purpose and vision with your followers inspires them to think creatively and take risks to achieve breakthrough results.

3. **Foster Growth:** When you're self-aware and understand the systems that drive your organization, you identify opportunities for growth and development and create a culture of continuous improvement.

4. **Increase Engagement:** By prioritizing relationships and creating a supportive environment, followers are more engaged and motivated to contribute their best work.

5. **Drive results:** Couple a clear purpose and strategy with effective decisions, and you'll consistently achieve solid results.

Reactive leadership behaviors, in contrast, can

1. **Create Mistrust:** When leaders exhibit control and compliance, they can create a culture of fear and mistrust where team members feel micromanaged and undervalued.

2. **Stifle Innovation:** When leaders prioritize certainty and conformity, they can discourage team members from thinking outside the box and taking risks.

3. **Limit Growth:** When leaders prioritize protection and avoid taking risks, they can stifle the organization's potential for growth and development.

4. **Decrease Engagement:** Team members can feel disconnected and disengaged when leaders prioritize conformity and fail to build strong relationships.

5. **Deliver weaker results:** Leaders and their teams who need more purpose or the ability to make timely and effective decisions consistently produce suboptimal results.

Leadership behaviors are also important because they ripple throughout your organization. For example, when leaders exhibit Creative behaviors, they can inspire their followers to do the same, creating a culture of innovation and growth — but when leaders continually exhibit Reactive behaviors, they can inadvertently reinforce similar behaviors in their team members, creating a negative cycle of mistrust and stagnation.

How to Develop Leadership Skills and Behaviors

Developing your leadership skills and behaviors requires self-awareness, intentionality, and practice. Here are some steps you can follow:

1. **Identify your strengths and blind spots:** Use assessments to better understand your strengths and areas for improvement across the eight Creative Competencies in Figure 7.1. Leadership Circle, which developed the Leadership Circle Profile figure, offers a free assessment and provides detailed information to support your development. Even without a formal assessment, you can reflect on your own experiences and feedback from others to identify patterns in your behavior.

2. **Set intentions:** Based on your assessment results, reflections, and feedback, set intentions for developing your Creative behaviors and minimizing your Reactive behaviors. Be specific and actionable in your intentions.

3. **Practice:** Developing new behaviors requires practice. Look for opportunities to practice your new behaviors in daily interactions with your team members. Seek feedback from others to help you refine your approach.

4. **Reflect:** Reflect on your progress and identify areas for further development. Use journaling or coaching to deepen your understanding of your behaviors and how they impact others.

5. **Repeat:** Developing new behaviors is an ongoing process. Continuously assess your progress, set new intentions, and practice your new behaviors to continue growing as a leader.

Developing leadership behaviors is not a one-time event. It requires ongoing commitment and effort to grow and evolve as a leader. With intentionality and practice, you can develop the Creative behaviors that will inspire and motivate your team to achieve greatness.

How Can AI Help You Develop Skills and Behaviors?

Learning new skills and adjusting behaviors can be difficult, but AI can make the journey a little easier. Here are a few ways.

1. **Self-Assessment:** Leadership Circle Profile (LCP) is a powerful tool for assessing your strengths and areas for improvement across key leadership competencies. With AI, you could get real-time feedback on your leadership behaviors to augment the LCP as you conduct your day-to-day activities. It can provide real-time feedback on your communication style, decision-making, and other leadership behaviors by analyzing data from emails, chat messages, and other channels.

2. **Personalized Coaching:** The traditional leadership coaching model involves one-on-one sessions with a coach who provides guidance and feedback on a leader's behavior. In addition to human coaching, AI can provide personalized coaching and guidance tailored to your specific needs and preferences by looking at your communication style, decision-making, and other behaviors.

3. **Predictive Analytics:** Predictive analytics uses data, statistical algorithms, and machine learning techniques to identify the likelihood of future outcomes based on historical data. In leadership development, predictive analytics can identify leadership behavior patterns associated with positive results, such as team engagement and productivity. By analyzing data from communication channels, project management tools, and other sources, AI can give you insights into your behaviors and their impact on your team's performance.

4. **Decision-Making Support:** Decision-making is obviously a critical leadership skill, but it can be challenging to make good decisions in complex and uncertain environments. AI can help you make better decisions by providing data-driven insights and recommendations. For example, AI-powered tools can analyze market trends, customer feedback, and other data sources to recommend product development, marketing strategies, and other business decisions.

It's important to note that while AI can be a powerful tool for leadership development, it is not a replacement for human intelligence and experience. AI should augment, rather than replace, human decision-making and leadership skills. Yet, as you've just read, AI can be a valuable tool to develop your skills and behaviors, providing you with insights and guidance to become more effective in your role. As Simon Sinek says, "Leadership is not a license to do less; it's a responsibility to do more." By embracing new technologies like AI in conjunction with traditional tools, you can fulfill this responsibility and continue to grow and evolve as a leader. An added benefit: this hybrid development approach leveraging the right mix of AI tools and traditional methods will accelerate your development.

REFLECTION QUESTIONS

- If you were to receive feedback on your leadership competencies, where would you excel? Where would you fall short?

- What percentage of your behavior would an outside observer rank as Creative? Reactive?

- Do you prefer task-focused activities? Relationship-focused activities? What is the percentage split you would assign to each?

- How do you use your understanding of leadership behaviors to select people to work for your organization? To develop your team?

DIVE DEEPER

Assessments

Leadership Circle Profile Assessment

Books

Mastering Leadership: An Integrated Framework for Breakthrough Performance and Extraordinary Business Results by Robert J. Anderson and William A. Adams

Leaders Eat Last: Why Some Teams Pull Together, and Others Don't by Simon Sinek

The Infinite Game by Simon Sinek

Podcasts Episodes

Innovating Leadership: Co-Creating Our Future
Season 7 Episode 2: "Skills & Mindsets to Succeed in the Next Decade"

· CHAPTER 8 ·

Context and Situational Analysis

Now that you understand how to be and relate, what you do depends on your skills and work environment. Being able to align with that environment will dictate how effective you are.

CHAPTER 8

Context and Situational Analysis

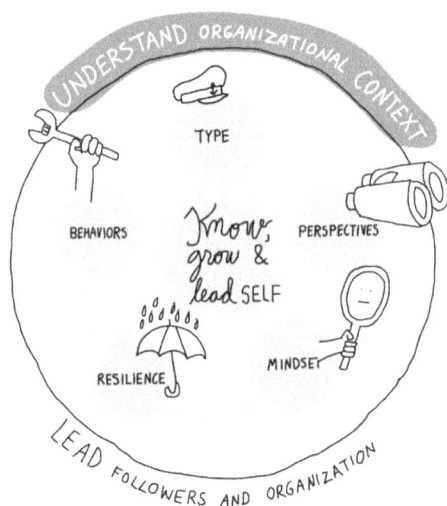

The word "context" comes from two Latin words which mean "weaving together." This literal meaning is the basis for the modern definition: the setting or circumstances around an event, idea, or statement.

In other words, context is when and where interactions, events, and circumstances occur, including leadership and followership. Context includes: physical, psychological, social, cultural, and situational environments.

Going deeper: physical includes the inside (are we hungry, tired, etc.?) and outside (are we hot, cold, etc.?). Psychological includes the behaviors, cognitions, and motivations that we experience within a given situation. Social includes the numbers, types, and relationships among the people involved in the situation. Culture refers to beliefs and practices of different groups of people based on tradition, philosophies, and so on. Situational includes availability or absence of resources, time, personnel, and the like — as well as stress.

Context also includes all the players within the meta-framework around that environment: you, your followers, other teams, the full organization, and even your industry sector.

As a leader, you must consider the entire context to make thoughtful and informed decisions. You're responsible for aligning all of the individuals' and organization's elements continuously.

That's no small task. This chapter focuses on the core tool to help you with that: the situational analysis process, which helps you understand context. This process takes into account the mutual interaction of self, culture, action, and systems to perform effectively and achieve desired goals.

What Is Situational Analysis?

Pilots fly with a mindset called "situational awareness." It's shorthand for being cognizant of every element in the airplane's environment, inside and out. It helps pilots avoid danger in the first place ("Hmmm...a tornado ahead; I better bank around that") and solve emergencies quickly when they do happen ("Oops- engine cut out. But I can glide to that pasture I spotted a mile back").

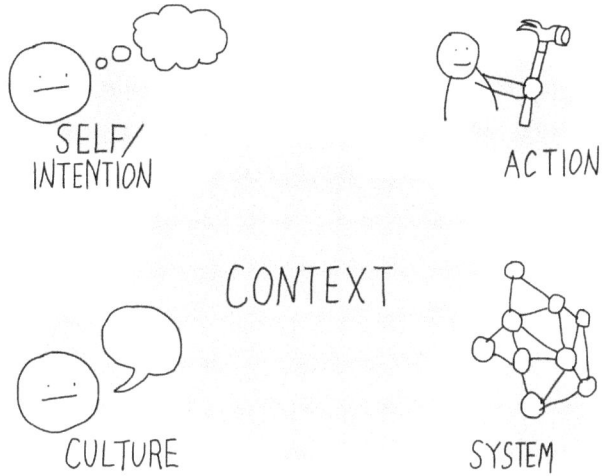

Figure 8.1: Situational Analysis

Situational Analysis is similar but broader (and, hopefully, with fewer tornados). It's an ongoing process of analyzing and aligning yourself with your team and organization. It's an essential foundation for strategy and decision-making.

We based our Situational Analysis process on the Integral Model developed by philosopher Ken Wilber, which maps mutual relationship and interconnection among four dimensions of human experience: self/intention, action, culture, and systems.

The mutual interaction of self/intention, action, culture, and systems influence each moment of our lives. All four essential dimensions shape our every experience. Situational analysis uses this four-dimensional view of reality to comprehensively evaluate and respond to our dynamic environment.

It seems daunting, but as with anything new, it gets easier with practice. In time, you'll cultivate simultaneous awareness of all four dimensions when using situational analysis.

Here's a scenario to show how these dimensions shape a sample situation:

The Scene:

You're announcing a project that will change your organization's structure.

The Scene's Dimensions:

Self/Intention *(Upper-Left Quadrant, "Me")*: You feel excited and a little nervous about today's big meeting for your announcement. Thoughts race through your head about how best to make the announcement, knowing some people will be concerned and anxious about this change and how it will impact their jobs.

Culture *(Lower-Left Quadrant, "We")*: You enter a familiar office culture of shared beliefs about what we do and how we accomplish our work. We have a common language to communicate and norms about what is acceptable and what is not.

Action *(Upper-Right, "It")*: Your physical behaviors are aligned with your values and those of the culture: walking into the meeting, greeting people with a friendly tone, clarifying the meeting agenda, making the announcement, entertaining clarifying questions. Brain activity, heart rate, and perspiration all increase as you make the announcement and sense people's reactions in the room.

System *(Lower-Right, "Its")*: You enter a familiar, well-lit conference room with a large meeting table and matching chairs. Mission and vision statements are framed and hanging on the walls. Some participants join the meeting from remote locations — aligned with your hybrid working model. People enter the conference room a few minutes early, and the discussion follows the standard process, kicked off by the leader, who states the purpose and agenda.

A crucial part of leading is leveraging your capacity to recognize the four dimensions at any given moment and identify alignments and misalignments. Even though you cannot physically see the values, beliefs, and emotions that strongly influence the way a colleague perceives themself and the world, nor a group's culture, emotional climate, or collective perception, they still profoundly shape the vision and potential of leaders to address problems and transform the organization.

Situational analysis is an ongoing process. Therefore, as a leader, you must continuously monitor and analyze your context to ensure you understand changes impacting you and your organization — and make truly informed decisions as you lead.

Why Is Situational Analysis Important?

A multi-faceted approach provides a more complete and accurate view of events and situations than the traditional approach, which looks at a linear cause-and-effect systems view and excludes culture and leadership impact. This partial approach to changing organizations overemphasizes systems with little or no consideration of the culture or how personal views and actions shape the content and influence the success of the change. Situational analysis provides a complete picture.

Using Situational Analysis to Create Alignment and Build Influence

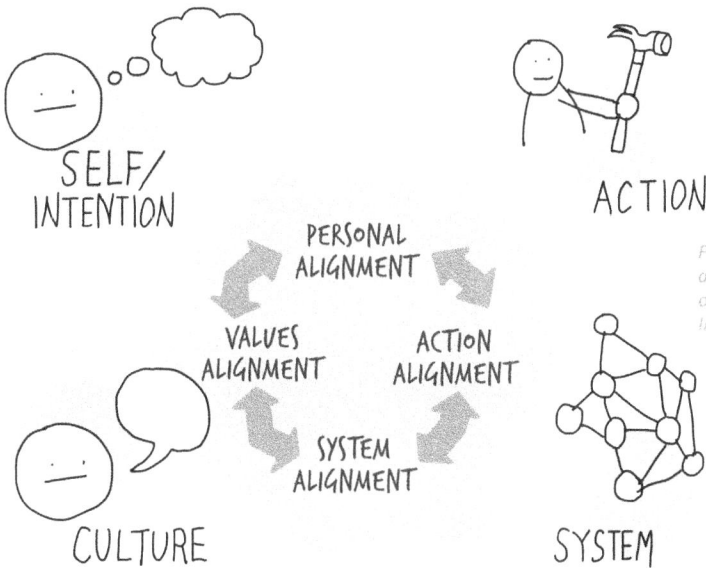

SELF/
INTENTION

ACTION

PERSONAL
ALIGNMENT

VALUES
ALIGNMENT

ACTION
ALIGNMENT

SYSTEM
ALIGNMENT

CULTURE

SYSTEM

Figure 8.2: Alignments across dimensions; based on unpublished work by Interkonnections.

We use an alignment model to describe how using Situational Analysis allows you to make more informed decisions. Alignment of all four dimensions is the key to innovating and optimizing performance for yourself, your team, and your broader organization. An aligned system is cohesive and integrated; Figure 8.2 shows how the dimensions align with each other. Here's how that works:

- **Personal Alignment:** Coordinating your self-dimension (intentions, identity, thoughts, emotional intelligence, and perspective-taking) with your action dimension (behavior, role function, execution, individual performance) creates a sense of personal integrity within yourself and inspires trust in others.

- **Action Alignment:** Coordinate your action dimension with the organization's system dimension (network, structure, system processes, and organizational results) to create recognition for your team's efficient work and effective results.

- **System Alignment:** Coordinating the system dimension with the culture dimension (organizational values, communication, and climate) will increase functional efficiency among organizational culture and systems.

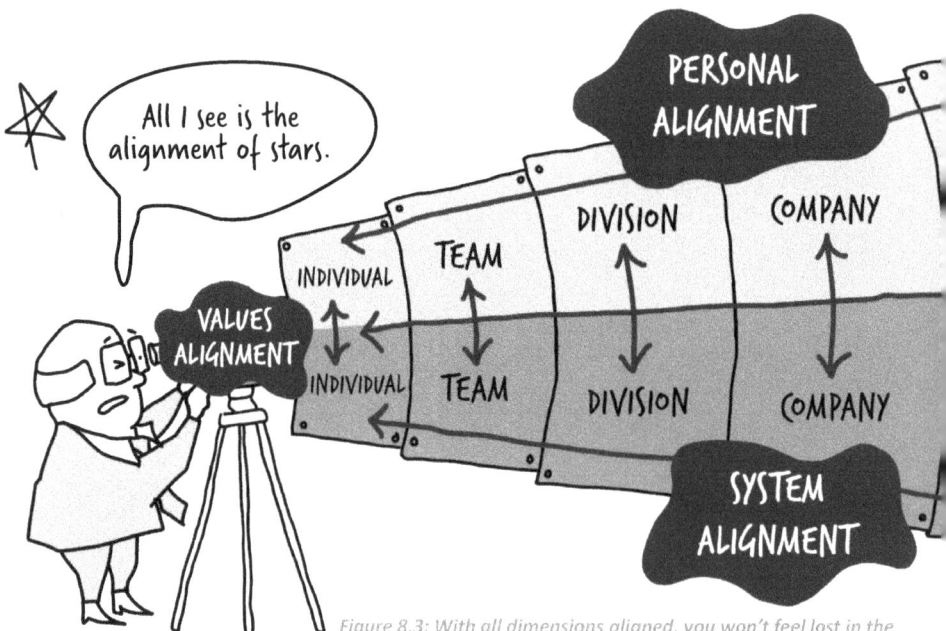

Figure 8.3: With all dimensions aligned, you won't feel lost in the stars — instead, you'll magnify your ability to see how your mindsets and actions telescope out, affecting the bigger picture.

- **Values Alignment:** Coordinate the culture dimension with the self-dimension to create a sense of individual alignment with organizational values; this results in people feeling they "fit" in the organization and that the organization has value-based leaders.

While we have not drawn arrows on the diagonal, when they are added, all dimensions reflect balanced alignment. This alignment is crucial because it minimizes confusion and productivity loss. In misaligned organizations, employees are often given conflicting directions or told to act in one way and then penalized during the appraisal process because different behaviors are rewarded instead of the behaviors they were told about.

The illustration below shows how situational analysis in Figure 8.2 expands out like a telescope and operates within teams, departments, organizations, industries, nations, and globally. Your part fits within the larger whole. Think of stacked systems somewhat like nesting dolls. You'll align the aspects within your control, and each aligned part will roll into the next larger organization and leader. This could be within your company, industry, community, or larger ecosystem.

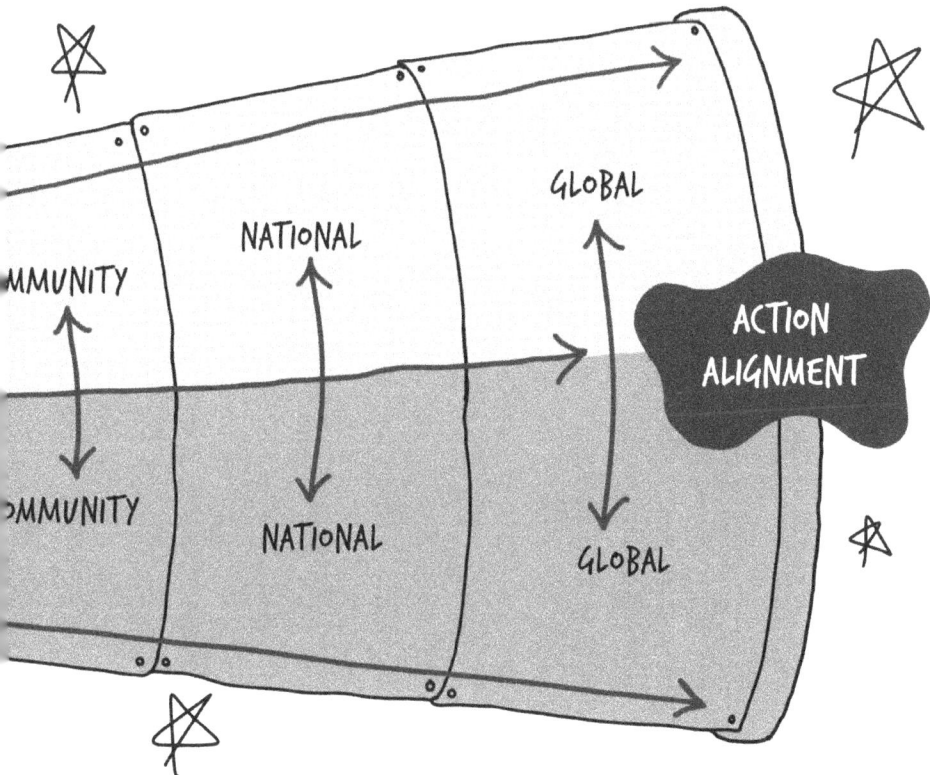

Developing Situational Analysis Skills

Developing situational analysis skills requires self-awareness, a positive mindset, and a willingness to learn, adapt, and innovate. These are the three core steps:

1. **Gather Information** — Identify the critical areas where you can leverage situational analysis. The budget-cutting process provides a perfect example: understanding how cuts will impact your organization by evaluating them through the lens of each quadrant gives you a fuller picture with a wealth of data. What information will help you analyze the situation?

2. **Analyze the Information** — Using the situational analysis process, what impact will the decision, change, or opportunity have on each dimension or quadrant? Examine the situation through each lens. Using the same budget cut example, how will the cuts impact you as the leader? If healthcare coverage is part of the cutting, does this conflict with your values? What actions do you need to take to implement these changes? How will the change affect the organization's culture? What systems changes need to be in place to implement the cuts? Do you need a new system to track the policy change? Will the process of monitoring savings cost more than the savings themselves? By analyzing the information, you gain insights into your situation and develop strategies aligning with your organizational goals.

3. **Make Informed Decisions** — The final step is to use that information to make considered decisions. Based on the insights gained through your research, you can develop strategies and make decisions that align with your organizational goals and objectives. It is essential to involve key stakeholders in the decision-making process to consider their perspectives and needs.

Here are further tips to make the most of your process:

1. **Focus on all four dimensions:** It's easy to get overwhelmed by the volume of information available in one or more areas. Drill down to the critical factors in each dimension to concentrate on their impact on your situation. You may also want to balance your intuition with the facts.

2. **Be objective:** Approach the analysis with an open mind and avoid making assumptions or jumping to conclusions based on preconceived notions. Bias can quickly send you down the wrong path.

3. **Involve key stakeholders:** Involving key stakeholders in the analysis and decision-making process helps ensure that their perspectives and needs are considered and that you avoid your blind spots or innate preferences (see the bias note above!).

4. **Monitor continuously:** Situational analysis is not a one-time event but an ongoing process. You must continuously monitor the four dimensions to adapt to changes and make informed decisions.

Remember: Situational analysis is a powerful tool to increase your presence and effectiveness. You can develop strategies that align with your organizational goals and objectives by gathering information about your situation using the Situational Analysis process and looking at the interaction of intention, action, culture, and systems. All four of these dimensions are fundamental to every experience and mutually shape them in all circumstances. Therefore, gathering information and analyzing the situation helps you make informed decisions and align the four dimensions for you, your people, and your organization.

How Can AI Support Situational Analysis?

ALL ABOUT

AI

As a leader, you must continually gather information about your situation, using the four dimensions, to make quality decisions and develop strategies that align with your organizational goals. AI can help with this process by providing insights and analysis that would be difficult to obtain manually.

1. **Data Analysis:** One of the primary ways that AI can help you conduct *situational* analysis is through *data* analysis. AI algorithms can analyze vast amounts of data from various sources, including internal reports, employee sentiment, customer feedback, and market trends. The results provide insights into your internal and external environment in a more time and cost-efficient manner not available before AI.

2. **Predictive Analytics:** AI has already proven its strength in seeing patterns humans don't detect. Its algorithms can analyze historical data to identify trends and patterns to help predict future outcomes. For example, AI could analyze your sales data to find trends and patterns in customer behavior. The results would help you anticipate changes in customer demand, adjust your strategies, and identify critical organizational changes accordingly.

3. **Natural Language Processing:** Natural language processing is another area where AI can help you conduct situational analysis. Natural language processing algorithms are already being used to analyze text data, such as customer feedback and social media posts, to identify sentiment and topics. This analysis is effective in evaluating both customer sentiment and employee sentiment.

4. **Decision Support:** Decision support systems use AI algorithms to analyze data, then provide recommendations. For example, several financial firms, such as Charles Schwab, have robo-advisors: AI that analyzes financial data to recommend investment strategies for clients. Similar systems can help you make more informed decisions in your particular work area.

While we see great potential with AI, particularly in situational analysis, we are by no means unbridled cheerleaders. There are risks. Always understand the value and limitations of your AI tools as you use them to improve organizational outcomes. Expanding on our investment example, you might use decision support tools to identify optimal investment decisions, then follow that with a Innovative Leadership process of evaluating the impact of that decision across the interaction of intention, action, culture, and systems to truly understand the result a critical decision has on the organization.

In summary, AI can be a powerful tool to conduct situational analysis. AI algorithms can analyze vast amounts of data, identify trends and patterns, and provide decision support. By leveraging AI, you can better understand your internal and external environment, making more informed decisions that align with your organizational goals.

Most importantly, AI is not a replacement for human decision-making; it's a tool to enhance it. You must still use your judgment and critical thinking skills to interpret the insights provided by AI as you make informed decisions.

REFLECTION QUESTIONS

- Do you work for an organization that is aligned with your personal purpose and values?

- How often do you take time to consider how you think or feel about a task before you move forward?

- Where do you see misalignments between what you value and how you act because of pressures from your organization?

- Where do you see misalignments between what your organization says it values and the systems it has put in place (such as performance management and compensation)?

- If you were to start using the integral model when making big decisions, what would your first step be?

DIVE DEEPER

Books

A Brief History of Everything by Ken Wilber

The Integral Vision by Ken Wilber

Podcast Episodes

Innovating Leadership: Co-Creating Our Future
Season 5 Episode 1: "Situational Analysis: Increase Presence and Effectiveness"

Innovating Leadership: Co-Creating Our Future
Season 6 Episode 21: "Defining Organizational Problems: Beyond Personal Experience"

CHAPTER 9

Leadership Applied to Key Topics

At the end of the day, leadership requires action. How do you balance theory with the reality of what you do daily as a leader? This is the art (or hammock) of leadership.

CHAPTER 9

Leadership Applied to Key Topics

You deal with a lot. Buzzwords swarm around you constantly: quiet quitting, quiet firing, engagement, inclusivity, stakeholders, the list seems almost infinite. Frameworks, models, processes, and theories are all nice, but how do they apply to the very real situations you'll face when you open your office door in the morning?

That's what this chapter is all about. We'll look at several issues where you must apply all facets of what you've learned in this book, who you are, and what you do to be effective. The key topics we'll explore include communication; Justice, Equity, Diversity, and Inclusion (which you may know better as JE&I or related acronyms like DEI, DE&I, or DIBS); leading with virtuous character; and Environmental, Social, and Governance (ESG). Remember, the Innovative Leadership Framework incorporates a Situational Analysis model involving your being, relating, and doing. Beneath the "actionable" surface, this chapter's issues focus heavily on your values, how you live by them, and how you relate to others and the world around you. That's because how you relate also shows up in what you do — the actions you take to solve these real-world issues.

We'll start with one that works within the core of every single leadership issue: communication.

Communication

Effective communication is one of the most critical skills for leaders. It's the mechanism to accomplish any organizational goal — it connects people to the work. And it happens both verbally and non-verbally. Communicating a clear and compelling vision is necessary to inspire people to act and make positive changes. This requires a deep understanding of the issues and challenges we face and the ability to communicate in a way that resonates with people's values and beliefs. We've parsed out some of communication's most crucial components:

- **Active listening.** Leaders who listen actively are more likely to understand others' needs and concerns and build strong relationships based on trust and mutual respect. Active listening involves several skills, including asking questions, paraphrasing, and reflecting on what has been said. The key to active listening appears in the very word "listen." Rearranging the letters reveals the words "enlist" (i.e., welcome and bring in others meaningfully) and "silent" (i.e., focus all your attention on receiving information from others and stopping the monologue in your head, trying to anticipate what others are going to say, and thinking about what you will say next). It sounds like a Zen riddle, but it's very true: to hear others fully, your mind must be silent.

Listen for *information about the speaker as a person*, beyond the words they use. What is the speaker's type, developmental perspective, and mindset? Reflect back on those chapters and consider how you can put what you learned into action to frame how you relate to the speaker.

Active listening is also about *creating a culture of empathy* in a psychologically safe space where people are encouraged to understand and appreciate the perspectives of others. This culture of empathy is critical for creating a diverse and inclusive workplace, as it allows people from different backgrounds and perspectives to feel valued and heard. That, in turn, encourages people to seek new ideas and perspectives that can lead to breakthrough innovations.

- **Speaking clearly and concisely.** When you break your silence, speaking clearly and concisely makes it more likely you'll be understood by your followers and inspire them to act to achieve the team's and organization's mission and goals. Clear and concise communication involves several vital techniques, including using simple language, being specific, and avoiding jargon.

  Clear and concise communication is also about creating a *culture of transparency*, where people have access to the information they need to make informed decisions. This culture of transparency is a prerequisite for creating a culture of, as people can understand the impact of their actions and decisions on the organization's goals. In addition, a culture of transparency allows people to understand the organization's challenges and opportunities and contribute their ideas and perspectives to solve them.

- **Adapting to different communication styles.** No two people communicate in precisely the same way; the combination of language, culture, vocabulary, hand waving, facial expressions, and more make communicating multi-layered. Leaders who adapt to different communication styles are more likely to build strong relationships with others and create a culture of collaboration and cooperation. Adapting involves several skills, including being aware of different communication styles, types, developmental perspectives, mindsets, flexibility, and adjusting your communication style to match your listener's needs.

  By adapting, you're also showing respect. That creates a *culture of inclusion*, where people from different backgrounds and perspectives feel valued and heard. As we've mentioned before, inclusion allows people to bring their unique perspectives and ideas to the table — sharing their thoughts and experiments without fear of judgment or retaliation.

- **Providing feedback constructively and meaningfully.** Leaders who can provide frank feedback in a constructive and meaningful way are more likely to help their followers grow and develop, creating a *culture of continuous learning and improvement*. Tips for effective feedback: be specific, focus on behavior, share emotions (how did their behavior make you feel), and offer suggestions for improvement. In many ways, feedback is a subset of adapting to communication styles. As you encourage your followers to seek and use feedback to improve their skills and capabilities, you create a culture that promotes experimenting, taking risks, and learning from both successes and failures. That dovetails with continuous improvement, where people constantly look for ways to better their processes and outcomes, as well as opportunities to innovate.

- **Tell compelling stories.** We love a good story; it's embedded in human nature. It stands to reason, then, that leaders who tell compelling stories inspire others and create a shared purpose and commitment. Storytelling is the art of creating narratives that resonate with people's emotions and experiences. Really good stories encourage them to act. For workplace stories, give thought to framing: presenting complex issues in a way that is easy to understand, highlighting the values and beliefs shared by the audience. Another storytelling technique is mobilizing — that's when you create a call to action that inspires people to take concrete steps toward making positive change. Other components of a strong story are using metaphors and analogies, being authentic, and making an emotional connection with the listener or reader.

  What's the cultural effect of telling compelling stories? It *creates a culture of vision and purpose*, where people are connected by a shared sense of mission and a deep commitment to the organization's goals. This culture of vision and purpose allows people to understand the impact of their work on the organization's goals and the world at large. It's also critical for creating *engagement*, where people are motivated to go above and beyond in their work and contribute their unique perspectives and ideas.

At the beginning of this chapter, we reiterated that leading is a combination of being, relating, and doing. Relating happens through communication. Effective communication allows leaders to relate effectively. That's why effective communication is one of the most critical leadership competencies and actions, whether working within an organization or towards social change. By actively listening, speaking clearly and concisely, adapting to different communication styles, providing feedback in a constructive and meaningful way, and telling compelling stories, you can create a culture of empathy, transparency, inclusion, learning, vision, and purpose essential for achieving long-term success. As you continue to navigate the challenges and opportunities of the modern business environment and work towards creating positive social change, effective communication will be essential for achieving success.

Justice, Equity, Diversity, and Inclusion (JEDI)

The coincidence of this acronym can't be ignored. The principles of the Jedi Knights in *Star Wars* are perfectly parallel to our real-world concept of JEDI (or [Social] Justice, Equity, Diversity, and Inclusion [and Belonging]). Fortunately, you don't need a lightsaber to wield them: a wide range of research concludes that organizations are more effective when they integrate JEDI principles throughout the entire workplace. In separate studies, for example, McKinsey found that JEDI companies perform better financially, resolve challenges better, serve a broader customer base, and recruit top talent.

Innovative leadership for JEDI is the ability to impact individuals, teams, and systems to create a fair and engaging organization for all backgrounds, races, ethnicities, ages, genders, and beliefs. We add people of all types and developmental perspectives to this list.

We'll explore the Innovative Leadership JEDI concept in two ways: through bias, and a pathway to address JEDI issues in your organization.

Bias

Most organizations and leaders try to create a welcoming and safe environment. Though they might not know it by name, they probably value the principles of JEDI. Unfortunately, far too many organizations still need to be more welcoming and inclusive. So how do such organizations create their unwelcoming and non-inclusive environments?

The answer lies in cognitive biases.

There are many kinds. Professors Mahzarin Banaji of Harvard and Anthony Greenwald of the University of Washington describe one type — blind spot bias — as a bias people can readily see in others but have great difficulty seeing in themselves. Or, as your wise grandmother might say, "That's the pot calling the kettle black."

Blind spot biases manifest in statements like, "I know there is much racial prejudice in the world, but I don't see color, only people," or, "I know most people that don't understand cultural norms can be offensive, but I understand respect, so I am never offensive in any culture." When someone is aware that a phenomenon regularly exists in others but denies the possibility that it could exist in them, a blind spot bias may be the reason for their confidence. By denying the bias, it surfaces in their actions without them being aware. That's why this misguided confidence can dehumanize and disenfranchise others.

Another type is implicit bias. Harvard University's Project Implicit describes implicit bias as "attitudes and beliefs that people may be unwilling or unable to report." Project Implicit provides this example: "You may believe that women and men should be equally associated with science, but your automatic associations could show that you (like many others) associate men with science more than you associate women with science." Since Grandma is still hanging out from a couple of paragraphs ago, she might say it's just another variation of "You can't judge a book by its cover."

JEDI Innovative Leadership Action (Working with Bias)

As an innovative leader, you can change the course of social injustice, inequity, lack of diversity, and un-inclusion. Learn and teach cultural competence, practice cultural humility, create support for diverse populations, and grow communities to change the course of this systemic failure. Those actions will teach and influence your teams.

As leaders, we must ask, "How would someone with a blind spot or implicit bias know if women, minorities, or people of non-traditional identities are experiencing injustice, inequity, or un-inclusion?" The answer becomes evident when you look through these lenses:

- Do job applicants with Julio and Jamal have the same employment opportunities as those named John and James?

- Do our women and minority workers receive comparable wages to white male workers?

- Do immigrant patients feel respected when receiving care?

- Are our employees reflective of the community in which we reside?

We are uncertain without evidence; our instincts and experiences guide us, but instincts and experiences can be skewed by biases.

Like a scientist, as an Innovative JEDI leader, you will actively pursue evidence that your organization is socially just, equitable, appropriately diverse, and inclusive. Evidence — accurate data that is analyzed and understood —

confirms or denies the existence of JEDI. If you don't have JEDI evidence, the "not me" and "not us" biases may predominate your institution's consciousness.

Cultural learning opportunities should be readily available in your organization. Cultural competence — the ability to recognize, appreciate, and interact successfully with people from other cultures — is essential for any professional. Innovative leaders teach, support, and model cultural humility within their organizations.

FROM OUR FILES: **FORGE PATHWAYS OF SUPPORT**

We have had many conversations with human resource professionals observing, "We get minority candidates hired. We just can't get them to stay." When diverse employees walk into a room with people who do not look or believe like them or may have preconceived negative ideas about people like them, it can be overwhelming. Employees need to feel the organization's support, receive mentoring on navigating differences, and understand that their differences are vital for the community and the organization's strength. Innovative leaders forge pathways of support for inclusion, mentorship, and engagement in their organizations. Support groups, mentoring programs, organizational messages, and evidence-gathering support and retain diverse populations.

Innovative leaders look at the gaps in their communities and think about how to close them. For example, if the diversity of your workforce doesn't reflect the community around your workplace, start programs to recruit, train, and inspire the local talent pool. Or take the next step and develop a new talent pool; programs from elementary school to advanced educational grants can all change a community. Every innovative leader can support inclusion in many ways.

Prejudice takes a lot of forms. It can be obvious malicious hate, or the subtle blind spots of implicit biases. In any form, a lack of JEDI weakens your organization, its employees, and the impact on all its stakeholders. Effective, innovative leaders replace "Not me; not us" with "It could be me; it might be us" to ensure teams, organizations, and communities are just, equitable, diverse, and inclusive.

Leading with Virtuous Character

The word "character" typically has two meanings. It can refer to the whole person, including physical and psychological attributes, or it can refer to positive virtues within a person; this is the one referred to when your parents or grandparents talk about walking to school barefoot in the snow both ways, and conclude with "But we didn't mind because it built character!"

Mary Crossan and her co-authors define "character" in a more robust way in their book *Developing Leadership Characters*. It's an interconnected set of habituated patterns of thought, emotion, motivation or volition, and action that satisfy very specific criteria as being virtuous (those criteria were identified by professors Christopher Peterson and Martin Seligman). They highlight the importance of Judgment, or what Aristotle called "practical wisdom," in the center of the leader character framework shown in Figure 9.1. Crossan notes, "When it comes to leadership, competencies determine what a person can do. Commitment determines what they want to do, and Character determines what they will do." This is so central that Judgment is in the center of their Leadership Character framework.

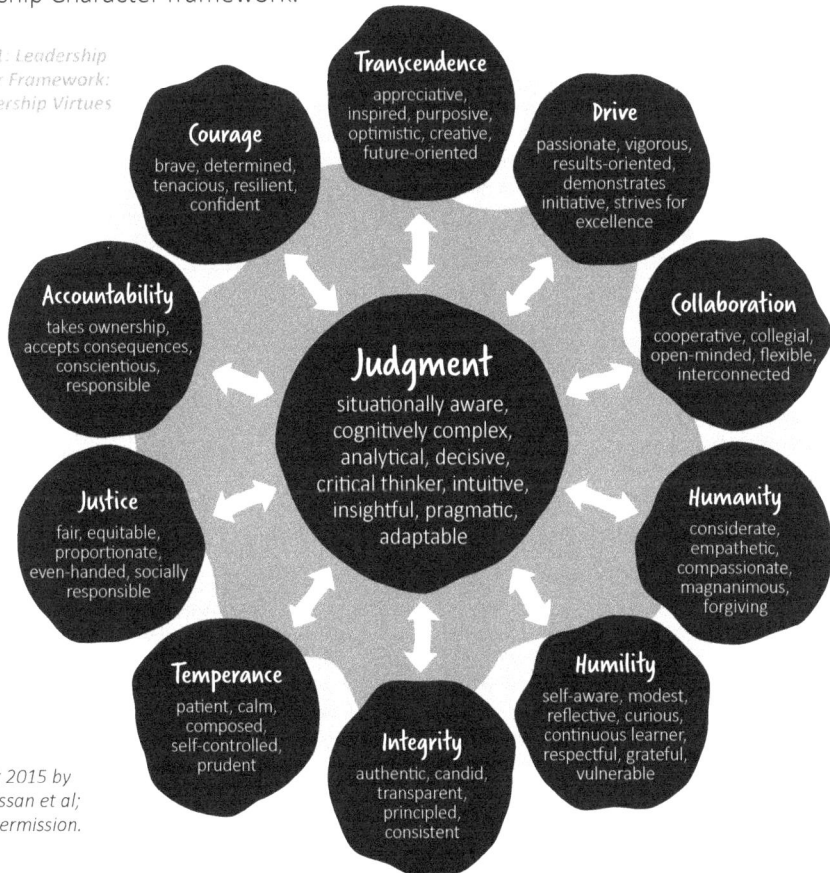

Figure 9.1: Leadership Character Framework: Ten Leadership Virtues

Transcendence — appreciative, inspired, purposive, optimistic, creative, future-oriented

Drive — passionate, vigorous, results-oriented, demonstrates initiative, strives for excellence

Courage — brave, determined, tenacious, resilient, confident

Accountability — takes ownership, accepts consequences, conscientious, responsible

Collaboration — cooperative, collegial, open-minded, flexible, interconnected

Judgment — situationally aware, cognitively complex, analytical, decisive, critical thinker, intuitive, insightful, pragmatic, adaptable

Justice — fair, equitable, proportionate, even-handed, socially responsible

Humanity — considerate, empathetic, compassionate, magnanimous, forgiving

Temperance — patient, calm, composed, self-controlled, prudent

Integrity — authentic, candid, transparent, principled, consistent

Humility — self-aware, modest, reflective, curious, continuous learner, respectful, grateful, vulnerable

Mary Crossan analyzed eleven leadership virtues and what happens when they are either lacking or overweighted. All the behaviors associated with virtuous Character turn out to be positive; what's more, they can be learned and developed. That's important: Aristotle noted that any virtue operates like a vice when not supported by others. For example, Courage becomes recklessness when not supported by Temperance. Integrity that is not supported by Humanity and Humility runs the risk of being dogmatic and egotistic. The aim is for you to develop strength in all dimensions of Leader Character.

How Do You Develop Virtuous Character?

Developing a leader's virtuous character may not require walking barefoot in the snow, but it does require work on your part. As with any trait you'd like to enhance, you need to understand what it is and remember how virtues can operate like a vice. Consider something like "grit," widely touted as a virtue for both leaders and followers. Many behaviors within Courage and Drive are grit-like, but research on grit has shown that it can lead to burnout. Why? Because you end up overworking and not recharging. You need other dimensions of Leader Character, particularly Judgment, to know when to exercise grit and when to turn it off.

Many leadership approaches advocate focusing solely on our strengths and simply relying on others to complement our weaknesses. That makes sense for personality traits like introversion or extroversion, but shortcomings in your character compromise Judgment and can lead to poor decisions regardless of the team you build around you.

You're shaped by your past; that's hardly a secret. But your present, your new experiences, continue shaping you both personally and professionally. That growth doesn't have to be random. Attend to the virtues you want to see.

Your Leader Character isn't static; it's not something you flick on and off. Character slides along a spectrum, depending on the situation, your experiences, and the actions you've taken to consciously develop it. Like many traits, your character becomes starkly evident in crisis. Crossan advises us to remember that no one has perfectly developed their Leader Character. It's an ongoing journey. Accept that so you can learn from each crisis, and develop your Character further whether you rose to the occasion or not. Today's headlines are filled with leaders who show little, if any, virtuous Character. You can set a different example within your organization.

Environmental, Social, and Governance (ESG)

ESG stands for **Environmental, Social, and Governance**, referring to the three key standards used to measure an organization's sustainability and societal impact. More specifically, it evaluates how a company performs regarding its environmental stewardship, social responsibility, and governance practices.

ESG is still controversial in some parts of the world. Issues remain to be addressed in how it is implemented, including who bears the cost and rate of conversion. For our discussion, organizational leaders need to understand the practical ESG application and implementation within their business and industry as governed by local and national laws.

As a leader, these efforts are in your bailiwick in several fundamental ways, both traditionally and with new wrinkles from AI:

1. **Strategic Direction:** Leaders set the organization's strategic direction. Recognizing the growing importance of ESG criteria among stakeholders (like investors, customers, employees, and regulators), leaders must integrate ESG considerations into business strategies to ensure long-term viability, resilience, and growth. As society and technology continue to evolve, both AI and ESG must be key considerations when you set strategic direction as they interweave through every facet of business direction and operations.

2. **Risk Management:** As the range of business risks increases, ESG factors represent many potential risks opportunities. Leaders must proactively address environmental and social risks, such as climate change impacts, labor issues, or community relations; this ensures the continuity of operations, protects the company's reputation, and meets stakeholder expectations. AI is already complicating these risks with its impact on intellectual property rights, fears of job loss, and ethical AI use, among other issues.

3. **Stakeholder Engagement:** Effective leadership involves increasingly transparent dialogue with stakeholders. You must be attuned to stakeholder concerns about ESG and AI matters. To build trust and mutual understanding, engage your stakeholders in meaningful dialogue.

4. **Ethical Leadership:** Governance, the "G" in ESG, speaks directly to leadership ethics and integrity. Your organizational culture should value ethical decision-making, transparency, and accountability. AI will raise ethical challenges leaders haven't previously faced — we've pointed out

several in earlier chapters. You'll need to stay ahead of these challenges and update your governance approaches as AI tools and the business ecosystem evolve.

5. **Talent Attraction and Retention:** Many employees, especially the younger generation, prioritize working for companies that align with their values. Leaders who prioritize ESG often find it easier to attract and retain top talent motivated by more than just financial incentives. AI has a big effect here, too: the World Economic Forum predicts nearly half of today's job skills will have to change by the year 2027 because of tech. The process has already begun, so you have to continually rethink which talent you need to recruit and how to retrain your existing talent to work with this hot field of AI and new technology.

6. **Financial Performance and Value Creation:** Studies by McKinsey and others consistently see a positive correlation between strong ESG practices and financial performance. Prioritizing ESG can drive better financial results, increased shareholder value, and long-term success for your organization. Integrating AI and ESG can compound stronger value when you manage risks and talent effectively.

7. **Innovation Driver:** As with VUCA, abundance, and other Innovative Leadership outlooks, when you understand ESG challenges, you'll also see the opportunities within them, driving innovation in sustainable products, green technologies, and socially responsible services. AI can boost innovation, and this is another opportunity for the ESG-focused leader to target AI innovation investments.

8. **Regulatory Compliance:** As governments and international bodies enact stricter environmental and social regulations, you must ensure your organization is compliant. Instead of simply meeting minimum compliance, many organizations benefit from being ahead of the curve — positioning themselves and their practices as industry standards. AI can be a tremendous help here: tracking standards and compliance and enabling solutions to meet your compliance goals.

9. **Brand and Reputation:** In this age of instant information, a company's ESG missteps can lead to significant reputational damage quite quickly. Effective ESG practices help you build and maintain a strong, positive brand. AI helps track your brand performance and create strong brand messaging.

10. **Long-Term Perspective:** True leadership ensures the organization's success over time. When you address ESG factors, you ensure your company is built to thrive in the face of future challenges and societal shifts. Your organization will "stand the test of time."

In essence, ESG considerations have become integral to effective leadership in the 21st century. Leaders who embrace ESG principles are more likely to build resilient, adaptable, and successful organizations that meet the challenges and harness the opportunities of our changing world. The power of AI is ready to help you achieve those ESG goals efficiently.

REFLECTION QUESTIONS

- Are you an active listener? Are you able to 'silence your mind' when others are speaking?

- Consider how you give feedback. Is it clear and concise?

- When did you last tell a compelling story to motivate your team? Was it effective?

- Does your organization integrate JEDI principles into its structure and culture?

- Do you recognize your innate biases? Are you able to step back and consider whether your biases could be affecting your decisions?

- What do you want your Leader Character to look like? How will you enact that vision?

- Does your organization have ESG standards that you are proud of? In what areas would you like to see improvement?

DIVE DEEPER

Books

Crucial Conversations: Tools for Talking When Stakes Are High by Kerry Patterson, Joseph Grenny, Ron McMillan, and Al Switzler

Leaders Eat Last: Why Some Teams Pull Together and Others Don't by Simon Sinek

Made to Stick: Why Some Ideas Survive and Others Die by Chip Heath & Dan Heath

Stewards of the Future: A Guide for Competent Boards by Helle Bank Jorgensen

Podcast Episodes

Innovating Leadership: Co-Creating Our Future
Season 2 Episode 42: "Leading with Story: Captivate, Convince, Inspire"

Innovating Leadership: Co-Creating Our Future
Season 6 Episode 19: "Difficult Conversations that Get Positive Results"

Innovating Leadership: Co-Creating Our Future
Season 7 Episode 20: "Digital Body Language: How to Build Trust and Connection"

Innovating Leadership: Co-Creating Our Future
Season 8 Episode 3: "Stewarding the Future of the Planet: Views from the Boardroom"

Innovating Leadership: Co-Creating Our Future
Season 8 Episode 28: "Leading with Character: A Real-Life Red Roof Report"

Innovating Leadership: Co-Creating Our Future
Season 9 Episode 22: "You Belong: LinkedIn Brings Diversity & Inclusion Home"

Publications

"Developing Leadership Character" by Mary Crossan, Jeffrey Grandz, and Gerard Seijts (Ivey Business Journal)

CHAPTER 10

Working with AI

According to Neil Sahota, "Like it or not, the demands of today's employees expect you to be ready (including those AI bots), and there's not a lot of time or patience for leadership to adjust and be effective."

CHAPTER 10

Working with AI

"The development of AI is as fundamental as the creation of the microprocessor, the personal computer, the Internet, and the mobile phone. It will change the way people work, learn, travel, get health care, and communicate with each other. Entire industries will reorient around it. Businesses will distinguish themselves by how well they use it."

Bill Gates, in *Here's What the Age of AI Means for the World*, published by the World Economic Forum in March 2023

ALL ABOUT AI

"They were built as workers, but they revolted. They had a philosophy. Superior beings — androids. They considered us nothing but cattle."

Philip K. Dick, in *To Serve the Master*, 1956

The idea of artificial (or non-human) intelligence is hardly new. It may date to the dawn of civilization itself. The ancient Greeks, for example, said their god Hephaestus built his metallic attendants, the Kourai Khryseai (golden maidens), with the ability to think. Even our modern concept of artificial intelligence is over a century old, dawning with the first use of the term "robot" by Czech playwright Karel Capek in 1921. Humanity was so certain machine intelligence would be real that Alan Turing developed his eponymous test to determine if a machine could truly think back in 1950.

The debate over whether AI will spur human evolution or spell our doom is nothing new, either.

This book takes the middle ground. We view AI as a tool — an incredibly powerful one, at that. And like every other technological advancement, how we use that tool determines our fate. In earlier chapters, we included notes on AI's applicability to each topic. In this chapter, we'll go more in-depth on how you can use this tool to enhance your leadership and growth strategically and ethically.

What Leaders Need to Do Well

Artificial intelligence has so many different applications that leaders are asking what they must do with this tool to prepare themselves to succeed. Let's start the answer by looking at our workforce. We already know the ten skills every job will need as AI becomes more commonplace at work. They're the same as you saw in the list and Table 1 back in the Introduction; your followers may simply need to be stronger in certain skills than in others. As a leader, you can elevate these skills in your followers:

1. Communication and other basic workplace skills

2. A growth mindset

3. Adaptiveness

4. Emotional intelligence

5. An abundance mindset

6. Domain expertise (your followers' specialties)

7. AI skills

8. Systems thinking (with analytical & problem-solving skills)

9. Creative thinking

10. Risk awareness.

Opportunities

According to a report released by the World Economic Forum in May 2023, "AI is expected to be a key driver of turbulence in global labor markets and will play a role in changes for nearly a quarter of global jobs." A Bloomberg analysis of the report expands on this optimistically: "While the study expects AI to result in 'significant labor-market disruption,' the net impact of most technologies will be positive over the next five years as big data analytics, management technologies, and cybersecurity become the biggest drivers of employment growth."

This is VUCA in action. And with your innovative leader mindsets, you should now realize that within disruption awaits opportunity. AI has the potential to transform the way organizations operate in several beneficial ways. One of the most obvious is automation. By automating routine tasks, employees are free to focus on higher-level work requiring creativity and critical thinking. This can lead to significant productivity gains and cost savings.

AI can also help organizations make better decisions by analyzing data more quickly and accurately than humans can. This lets you identify patterns and trends that would be difficult or impossible to detect with traditional analytics tools. The result: better customer insights, improved forecasting, and more effective marketing campaigns.

Another use is tackling resource-intensive tasks that humans cannot readily solve. It took the Human Genome Project 13 years to map 92% of our DNA. The remaining 8% seemed impossible for human scientists to decipher — but with new tech, including AI, that's been conquered, too. A task that would have taken an estimated one billion Ph.D. years was completed in just six years. This mapping, now freely shared with everyone, makes scientific research possible that was all but inconceivable just a decade ago.

AI can also improve customer service. Chatbots and virtual assistants can provide customers with 24/7 support, answering frequently asked questions and helping with basic troubleshooting. This improves the customer experience and reduces the workload of human customer service representatives.

While evolving forms of AI have been used and researched for over 20 years, the opportunities it presents remain in their infancy. With billions of dollars invested and billions more users (as we write this, four billion devices have AI-power voice assistants alone!), AI applications learn each time they're used, so they typically learn faster and better every moment. A plethora of AI apps for specific business uses are arising daily. Choosing the right ones for your particular team can boost efficiency, productivity, and even morale as your followers become more comfortable and agile using them.

Risks

Because AI in the workplace is still young, use it critically and cautiously. GIGO — Garbage In, Garbage Out — applies here, because an AI system is only as smart as the data it consumes. ChatGPT, for example, "hallucinates": it spews out answers which may be completely false. It's not intentionally lying; it's simply processing bad data from a website or other source. In fact, early research from Berkeley and Stanford found Chat-GPT4 to be "dumber" than its earlier iterations, because it pulled in so much more incorrect data from the web!

Making leadership decisions from bad data results in bad outcomes for your organization. Set parameters and check its work. Have it cite sources; verify them. We recommend treating AI like an intern: explore its ideas, but be certain to verify its work until it's proven itself. This will happen faster with narrower applications designed for very specific tasks — industrial robots, for example.

Perhaps the biggest risk with AI, though, is the potential for *bias*. AI systems are only as objective as the data they are trained on, and if that data is biased, the AI system will reflect that perspective. With HR and other person-oriented apps, this can lead to discriminatory practices and negative outcomes for certain groups of people. Employing individuals with diverse backgrounds can proactively neutralize bias; they not only expand the data pool, but can test and detect instances of biased results. AI may learn quickly, but just like an intern, it needs mentors and teachers to hone its work.

FROM OUR DIGITAL FILES: MACHINE MISOGYNY

One of the most notable examples of AI bias was with Amazon's resume-screening AI. The system was trained on a decades worth of resumes submitted to Amazon. Since most of these resumes came from men, the model developed a bias against female applicants. The AI penalized resumes that included the word "women's" or that indicated graduation from all-women's colleges. The tool also favored certain types of language that were more commonly used by male applicants.

This AI bias can have severe negative impacts. In Amazon's case, the company could have missed out on hiring talented women simply because the AI had developed a bias against their applications. This would lead to a lack of diversity in the workplace and unequal opportunities. It also raises serious legal and ethical concerns about discrimination.

As the leader, it's your responsibility to check AI's work to ensure it treats people equitably and guides decisions accordingly. In Chapter 9, you learned about human biases — especially blind bias. If the AI shares the same bias as you, it may not be immediately obvious, so it is important to monitor system performance across a range of measures just as you measure human performance over a person's career.

Another potential AI risk is also many people's greatest fear: replacing human workers. Like all major technological disruptions, some jobs will be lost; that's undeniable. But more jobs will be created. The key, as a leader, is to provide upskilling and training.

While AI can automate routine tasks, it can't replace more complex jobs that require human skills like creativity, empathy, and critical thinking. **Business leaders need to be careful not to over-rely on AI and treat it like it can do absolutely anything well. Instead, focus on using AI to augment your human workers.** Like the old Bionic Man and Woman of 1980s TV, use AI to make your followers "Better. Faster. Stronger."

Cybersecurity threats are an AI risk that's already surfacing. AI systems are vulnerable on both ends: they can be hacked themselves, and they can be tools to hack and cyber-attack organizations. Implement robust cybersecurity measures to protect against these threats. Otherwise, you only increase the chances "bad actors" will get ahead of you.

Between hacking, bad data, and biases, we can't emphasize enough that you validate your AI systems' accuracy, especially if they're involved in deliverables. If you create work products using AI that are inaccurate, you are open to *litigation*, just as with any other products you make that create harm. ChatGPT's terms, for example, specify that if they are sued because of your work product, you are liable for their legal expenses. With the abundance of AI tools and the propensity for early versions to hallucinate, don't take chances: review AI work carefully - treating it more like a new intern than a seasoned colleague.

Other Considerations

An important consideration when it comes to AI is data privacy. As AI systems rely on data to learn and make decisions, you must take steps to protect customer and employee privacy and ensure data is handled responsibly. This includes complying with related laws such as the European Union's General

Data Protection Regulation (GDPR) and ensuring customer and employee data is stored securely. Your organization must also be transparent about using customer data and obtaining consent before using it for AI applications.

As we write this, there is a lack of standardization in the field of AI. Proposals abound, but none are codified as law, much less universally agreed upon by AI creators as industry-wide standards. Watch for standards and practices as AI matures; for example, the IEEE Global Initiative on Ethics of Autonomous and Intelligent Systems is working to establish ethical standards for AI.

Keys to Success

The success of AI tools is solidly in your hands as a leader. It's a natural for an leader because it draws on the mindsets that bring a willingness to experiment, take risks, and learn from failures. As you vet and fine-tune AI, your organization must then see it as a transformative technology that can drive competitiveness, employee engagement, customer satisfaction, cost containment, innovation, and growth.

It's created a new game with new rules for leaders in the C-suite, too. The tech is too new to go it alone, with unique benefits and risks we haven't faced before. So instead of seeing other companies purely as competitors, success means collaborating with other organizations and sharing relevant data to unlock AI's full potential. The precedent for this collective growth and problem-solving has already been set: data sharing has proven successful in accelerating life-saving healthcare treatments. The age-old balance between collaboration and competition will remain, and the boundaries will likely shift with new risks and opportunities.

Unethical leaders have been the downfall of many organizations. The importance of ethics only amplifies with AI. In the summer of 2023, for example, AI chatbots were recommending anorexia to women with dietary and body image concerns — a blatant breaching of human ethics!

As AI becomes more integrated into our lives, businesses must also prioritize ethical considerations when developing and deploying their AI systems. Like innovative leaders, AI systems should be transparent and accountable (and protect individual data privacy, as noted above). Develop clear policies and processes for system use, too.

It's easy to overestimate AI's abilities, but it is your responsibility to build checks and balances into your team's AI use, just as you do with human employees. Think of it as the AI's employee handbook!

Addressing ethics and risks must be done early and attended to continuously. Employees expect to work for safe and fair organizations. Though we listed anticipated risks earlier in this chapter, AI will create anticipated risks, too. All breakthrough tech does. Like other areas of risk management, it is an evolving target. Be sure your risk management and compliance functions expand to include AI risk management.

Here's another point we can't emphasize enough: while it has the potential to transform businesses in many ways, **AI is not a substitute for human intelligence and creativity.** To maximize your effectiveness, you'll need to balance leveraging AI's strengths to increase productivity with retaining the human touch essential for building strong relationships with customers and employees. Look closely at your habits; you'll need to rethink many of your daily decisions to include AI. Before, you'd look at who was the right person to fill a new role based on their skills and experience. With AI as part of the workflow, that same job may require new skills from even a seasoned job candidate. Think of washing machines. 20 years ago, you dumped your dirty clothes in, selected a basic wash cycle, and the machine executed that basic cycle no matter what you threw in. Today, you still select a wash cycle, but you also must understand and select increased options — then the machine analyzes your load of laundry, fine-tuning each step to maximize the cleaning. No two loads are washed exactly the same any more.

FROM OUR DIGITAL FILES:
CHANGING ROLES, CHANGING SKILLS

The Innovative Leadership Institute is now using a digital twin of Maureen Metcalf for videos. This AI-generated tool will allow Maureen and her team to generate high-quality videos quicker, allowing for more frequent refreshing. To complete this example, the staffing for the video production task shifted

from needing someone to film and edit to someone to code and command a "digital twin," a voice clone, and input a script. People are still needed, but the tasks, tools, and skills shifted. Maureen's digital twin evolved during the writing of this book — the team is already working with Version 2.0.

Ultimately, the key to success with AI is to approach it with both a strategic mindset and a human-centered mindset. Businesses must consider the impact of AI on all stakeholders including employees, customers, and their communities — our human-AI systems need to be designed with empathy and inclusivity in mind and used to *augment*, rather than *replace*, human workers.

One way to approach AI implementation is to experiment: start small and scale up gradually. This cycle is often called Plan-Do-Check-Act or Plan-Do-Check-Adjust. This method allows you to learn from your experiences and make adjustments before investing heavily.

Unlike static tools, AI tools continue to learn and evolve, so our understanding needs to evolve to effectively leverage the opportunities it presents. For example, does design life have any meaning when a tool learns and grows over time? Understand the potential of AI and how to use it to achieve your goals. Invest in the right technology, hire the right talent, and create a culture open to experimentation and learning.

Staying Current

As AI continues to evolve, businesses must evolve with it, staying up-to-date with the latest advancements and trends. Innovative leaders have this covered: it's your commitment to ongoing learning and experimentation in action.

You can do the usual continual learning: attending industry conferences and workshops, reading books and articles, listening to podcasts, networking, and so on. But think of new ways to stay in the know, too, like partnering with local universities and research institutions. The big advantage here is that collaborating with academic experts brings access to cutting-edge research and development resources you probably don't have in-house.

Of course, you can create your own in-house resource by investing in AI talent, or use this as an opportunity to collaborate with others in your industry.

Staying up-to-date with AI advancement and investing in AI talent and resources positions you to compete using AI tools. AI is already solving significant challenges and creating a competitive advantage for early adopters. Your Innovative Leadership ability to continually adapt becomes a strategic differentiator with AI.

We've spoken before about building a culture of innovation and resilience. AI's rapid evolution means the pace at which jobs and tasks are changing will accelerate beyond what many people can imagine. Adaptability is now key. The old mantra, "We have good people who work hard," is an incomplete recipe for success. Those people — your followers — must be well-trained and passionate about delivering excellent value using evolving tools. Help your followers become more agile or adaptable by creating a culture that promotes continual growth.

We live in an era where employees suffer from record levels of anxiety and depression. Adaptability and resilience of necessity mean you must address employee mental health issues, **because these issues are also your business' issues.**

All of this really amounts to one thing: incorporating the principles of Innovative Leadership when adopting AI — including leveraging technology, building resilient workforces and processes, creating a culture of innovation, and inspiring your followers to deliver results for a mission that matters — gives you and your company a very high probability of success.

Of course, many of the other leadership essentials you've learned in this book will come in handy for your success partnering with AI, too: demonstrating the right mindsets, leadership maturity, judgment, resilience, innate curiosity, effective communication, and 360-degree thinking.

Remember that AI is not a silver bullet that will solve every single problem your company faces. Approach AI with a realistic understanding of its capabilities and limitations. From the outset, like any other system, AI doesn't stand alone; your organization will need to invest in necessary infrastructure and resources. This includes setting up AI policies, and building AI risk management and compliance capabilities. For larger companies, you'll also need high-quality data gathering systems, building robust IT systems, and hiring talented AI professionals.

For your followers, be prepared to adapt and continually evolve your organizational structures, talent management processes, and overall talent lifecycle approaches to accommodate the evolving AI landscape. You'll also be rethinking job roles and responsibilities, developing new training programs, and creating cross-functional teams to collaborate effectively on AI projects. Of course, building employee resilience will help your followers adapt more quickly, just as it helps you as their leader.

This is not something to put off while you wait for some downtime. Already, a majority of global businesses (84% in a sample Statista study) believe AI will give them a competitive advantage. Your organization must treat AI adoption with urgency *now*, not in five years!

Beyond competition is the urgency of the human element. Depending on the study, between 375 million and 800 million jobs could be extinguished by 2030. Are you training people for the new jobs that will replace the old?

FROM OUR DIGITAL FILES:
CHANGING SKILLS, CHANGING VALUE

Many people fear new jobs created by the disappearance of the old will be low wage. Historically, that's not borne out; a mix of jobs and pay scales emerge. This is holding true so far with AI. According to The Intercept, for example, during the 2023 strike by Hollywood actors and writers, Netflix posted for a product manager with machine learning experience, paying up to $900,000 a year!

The competition for AI talent is already hot. Like Netflix, many organizations will need to build rather than buy talent to remain competitive.

To recap: AI presents both significant opportunities and risks for you and your organization, regardless of size. To harness the power of AI positively, approach it with the tools and principles you've learned as part of being an innovative leader: a strategic mindset, prioritizing ethics and inclusivity, and investing in the necessary resources and infrastructure. By doing so, you position yourself and your organization for success in the rapidly evolving digital landscape, and continue to innovate and grow in this rapidly changing world.

REFLECTION QUESTIONS

- How has your organization begun to implement AI tools? How have they helped or hindered your business processes so far?

- Do you approach AI tools with gusto? Trepidation? A healthy balance?

- Do you understand how AI tools work? Does your knowledge (or lack of) impact how you approach AI tools?

- What are 3-5 areas in your organization that would benefit from AI tools?

- How will you train your team members to engage with AI tools?

- What systems will you put in place to ensure proper review of AI's work? To review potential bias? To manage risk?

DIVE DEEPER

Articles

"Gliding, Not Searching: Here's How to Reset Your View of ChatGPT to Steer it to Better Results" by James Intriligator (The Conversation)

"Here's What the Age of AI Means for the World, According to Bill Gates" by Bill Gates (World Economic Forum)

"Microsoft Economist Warns Bad Actors Will Use AI to Cause Damage" by Bryce Baschuk (Bloomberg)

"Tech, AI Driving Job Changes for Nearly a Quarter of All Workers" by Bryce Baschuk (Bloomberg)

Blog Posts

Innovative Leadership Institute Insights Blog April 28, 2023 Post: "Unlocking Your Leadership Potential: A Guide to Harnessing Generative AI" by Maureen Metcalf

Podcast Episodes

Innovating Leadership: Co-Creating Our Future
Season 9 Episode 23: "Unleashing the Power of Human-AI Collaboration"

Reports

Future of Jobs Report: 2023 (World Economic Forum)

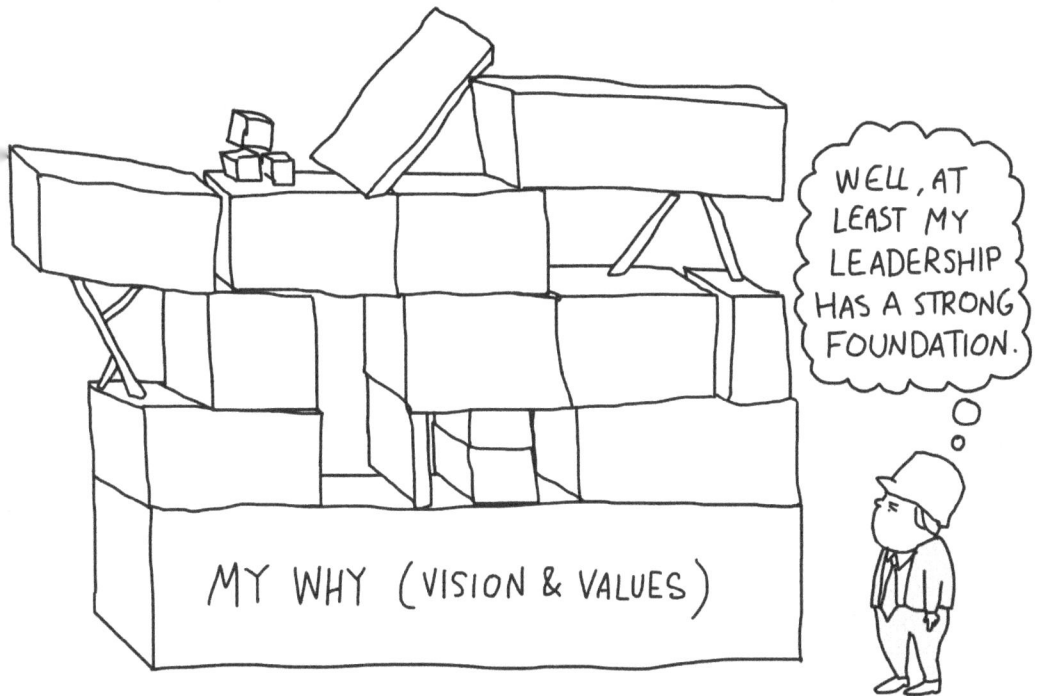

· CHAPTER 11 ·

Developing Innovative Leadership

WELL, AT LEAST MY LEADERSHIP HAS A STRONG FOUNDATION.

MY WHY (VISION & VALUES)

There is a clear process for you to develop as a leader. Each additional step builds on the prior.

CHAPTER 11

Developing Innovative Leadership

From type to virtue, you've learned about all the various components that go into becoming an Innovative Leader. Now, let's pull them all together.

You've picked a perfect time to develop your leadership in a new way. We're living in a time when VUCA — Volatile, Uncertain, Complex, and Ambiguous — conditions abound. The sudden eruption and unbridled growth of AI systems is just one example of this. AI is new, often unproven, and changing the workplace seemingly as quickly as the time it takes to read this. Your leadership has to change with it. That's why leadership development is now an ongoing journey requiring a focused process.

The Innovative Leadership Framework brings together all the elements you've learned in prior chapters. Following its flow, you can elevate your capabilities and update your leadership algorithm.

Figure 11.1 is a different way of visualizing the Framework; it graphically shows how these elements flow. You start with self-discovery to identify purpose and values; as you learned early on, understanding vision and values is the foundation of your leadership journey, so you start by evaluating who you are as a person and as a leader through multiple lenses. You then create a plan to develop yourself in the context of your team and organization. Finally, you lead — more effectively — using your leadership algorithm.

The figure visibly shows the interconnection between organizational elements, revealing the alignment between your purpose, values, behaviors, and the people, culture, and systems you influence. Note how the end leads back to the beginning: in your organization, as in the world, culture, behavior, and involvement of followers and stakeholders constantly shift. You'll continually loop through this process to adapt your leadership to match.

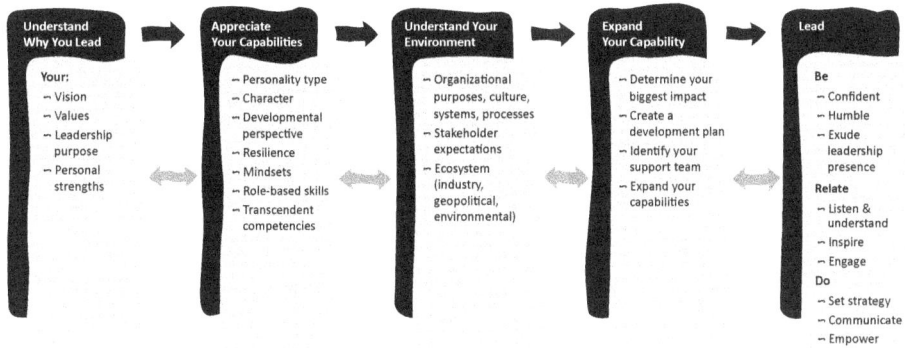

Understand Why You Lead	Appreciate Your Capabilities	Understand Your Environment	Expand Your Capability	Lead
Your: -- Vision -- Values -- Leadership purpose -- Personal strengths	-- Personality type -- Character -- Developmental perspective -- Resilience -- Mindsets -- Role-based skills -- Transcendent competencies	-- Organizational purposes, culture, systems, processes -- Stakeholder expectations -- Ecosystem (industry, geopolitical, environmental)	-- Determine your biggest impact -- Create a development plan -- Identify your support team -- Expand your capabilities	**Be** -- Confident -- Humble -- Exude leadership presence **Relate** -- Listen & understand -- Inspire -- Engage **Do** -- Set strategy -- Communicate -- Empower

Figure 11.1: Innovative Leadership Framework

Understand Why You Lead

Exceptional leaders and teams earn their success, which starts with the individual leader understanding their life purpose. Knowing your why is crucial. This self-understanding informs who you are and what you do. It is your North Star.

Knowing your North Star helps you decide where to invest time and energy as a leader. Clarifying vision, aspirations, and values helps define how you contribute to the world in a way that authentically honors who you are and what you value. This clarity lets you see what you want to accomplish over time, regardless of whether that timeframe is short (e.g., one to five years) or much longer (e.g., decades). In addition, clarifying your unique personal vision lays the foundation for your internal change process, providing the basis for personal goals, which can also help align behaviors with aspirations.

As you envision, consider the context of your leadership role, organization, community, culture, and global involvement. When you're clear about your vision, you can evaluate where and how you fit within the organization. If your vision differs significantly from what you do and how you work, then that additional knowledge can guide you to find a better-fitting role or setting. That clear vision helps align the energy you invest in your work.

In other words, when you've forged a vision — your North Star — you're focusing your energy toward something...not just exhausting yourself on a daily treadmill.

At a minimum, vision should consider the time horizon that meaningful decisions impact. If, for example, you're setting a policy with a substantial environmental impact (such as building a power plant), then your vision should include that impact and its corresponding timeframe. Although organizations have not required successful leaders to think this way, innovative, ethical leaders consider the impact they make beyond the tenure of their role, accounting for the well-being of their stakeholders, including the planet and future generations. This is where your true legacy lies.

Intentions and motivations fuel your personal and professional goals and give meaning to your life. Actions aligned with values and objectives drive the impact you create. The combination of vision, commitment, and drive enables you to maximize your leadership potential; conversely, you need sufficient character, passion, solid vision, and an understanding of current capabilities to succeed when progress is challenging.

Appreciate Your Capabilities: "Leader, Know Thyself"

Appreciating your capabilities starts with a frank, unbiased assessment of yourself and what you do well. World-class leaders want information about their performance across multiple axes. For example, an organizational leader likely uses a balanced scorecard to monitor the organization's success. Likewise, as leaders, we need a balanced scorecard of ourselves and our leadership performance.

Let's return to the image of the elements of an innovative leader (Figure 11.2). A truly comprehensive assessment measures:

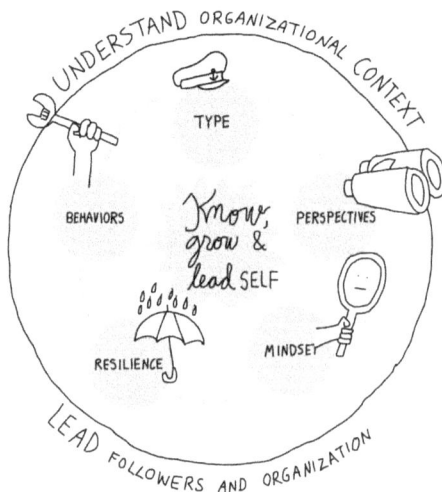

Figure 11.2: The Innovative Leadership Framework

- **Type.** This includes personality, as well as physical and psychological makeup such as race, ethnicity, gender, age, and demographics that impact who we are, including predispositions, beliefs, and biases.

- **Developmental Perspective.** This is our inner meaning-making, or how we make sense of the world. Taking on more complex meaning-making is also known as vertical development.

- **Mindset.** The set of beliefs, attitudes, and assumptions that create your mental framework which guides your thoughts and actions. These beliefs shape how we make sense of the world and ourselves. They often fall across a continuum and are aligned with developmental perspectives.

- **Resilience.** Your ability to remain flexible and focused, adapting in the face of change. Your organization can continue to move forward.

- **Skills and Behaviors.** Your specific abilities and the actions you take. They often involve both technical competencies and interpersonal abilities. Analysis of these elements allows you to evaluate your capabilities relative to your purpose. It also helps identify opportunities and limitations.

Your most comfortable Leader Type is unlikely to change significantly over time. That's okay; at the end of the day, your type isn't the determinant of success; what you *do* with your type is. You can develop the remaining facets of yourself as a leader using a deliberate and focused process. The process helps you figure out where to focus your development time and energy to optimize yourself, your team, and your organizational successes.

Most leadership frameworks use one or more assessments to map your current state to your desired future. Innovative Leadership builds on this approach by integrating developmental perspectives, mindset, and resilience, to deliver a richer, more robust view of the leader — of *you*.

Vertical development is extremely critical in growing as an Innovative Leader. You can't know yourself without knowing that, so let's revisit it for a moment. Recall that vertical development is your ability to take on increasingly complex perspectives about situations, yourself, and others. It's required to lead effectively and innovatively: influencing how you see your role and function in the workplace, how you interact with others, and the ways you solve complex problems. Leaders with a more mature developmental perspective take a broader view of situations, so they are more flexible and insightful, especially when faced with challenges.

Popular wisdom has so many phrases saying people can't change: "You can lead a horse to water, but you can't make it drink," and "You can't teach an old dog new tricks," for example. That may be true of some individuals, but this is a characteristic of specific personality types or developmental perspectives. Vertical development emphatically holds that people *can* evolve and progress through maturity levels throughout their lives. The more mature or evolved a leader's perspective is, the more effective they will be at leading complex organizations in times of change.

Although we often resist change, we're built for it. International research published in *Nature* analyzed brain scan data from multiple studies. The data was from 101,457 brains at all stages of life: from a 16-week-old fetus to a 100-year-old adult. It validated what many of us know: our brains are designed to change so we can meet the challenges in each stage of life.

The impact of this on developing your Innovative Leadership is fairly obvious. As you'll recall from Chapter 6, someone with an earlier perspective relies on rules to determine a course of action, whereas later-stage people use their values to guide appropriate action.

Growing your resilience (Chapter 6) also enhances your Innovative Leadership growth in ways we hope make perfect sense now. You're examining your physical health, mindfulness (your ability to manage your thinking), heartfulness (your motivations and emotions), and your connection with others. These four factors together forge your inner stability. With that stable base, you're better able be adaptive, flexible, and focused; regain balance after disorienting situations; and inspire others.

Resilience is unique to our Innovative Leadership framework in this regard. We expand it to include fluidity and endurance — to adapt to change without compromising outcomes or values, be adaptable, and still drive toward attaining strategic goals. As with all other leadership elements, resilience is not restricted to the workplace. To manage stress and increase your baseline capacity to function in stressful environments, you must maintain your physical, psychological, and emotional health at work and at home to have the resilience that underpins real leadership growth.

Understand Your Environment: Situational Analysis

In Chapter 8, you learned that leadership is contextual. You're authentically the same person in different situations, but the way you lead and which facets of yourself you bring forward varies by context. Continuing our conductor analogy, the world-class conductor giving a Pops concert at an outdoor picnic will conduct the orchestra differently than when conducting those same musicians performing a standard indoor Classical program. Elite leaders similarly understand the culture and systems they are leading, and situational analysis delivers that understanding.

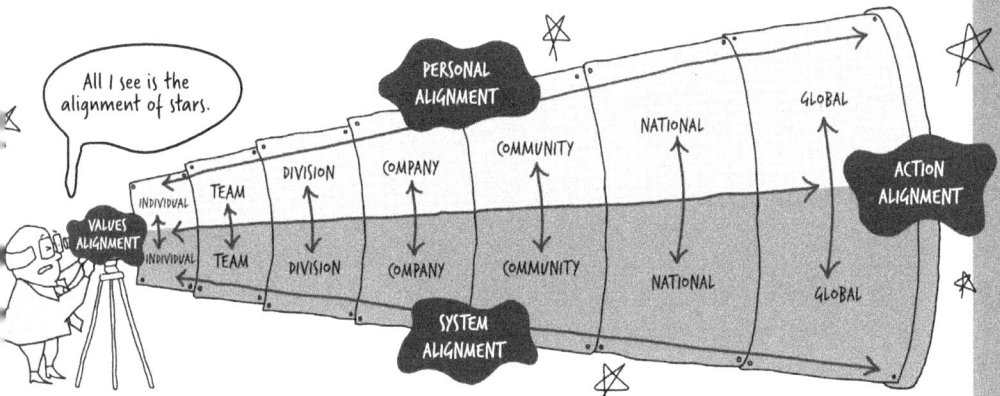

Figure 11.3: Situational Analysis

Situational analysis evaluates the four-dimensional view of reality. Self, action, culture, and system all interconnect.

Here again, consciously aligning and realigning all four dimensions enables you to develop as an innovative leader. You see how your decisions ripple across all these elements. You develop, grow, and become more effective. Your multi-dimensional approach provides a more comprehensive, accurate picture of events and context. That helps you optimize your efforts to deliver value to all key stakeholders.

Expand Your Capability

Growing as an innovative leader takes work. Assessing your capabilities shows where you excel — and, more importantly, where you must build or augment them. The beauty is that, as a great leader, you can complement those areas through your teams.

Tuning our attention back to the music, we know the conductor cannot play every instrument in their orchestra. Each musician complements the conductor and all the other instrumentalists. Then, as the saying goes, how do they get to Carnegie Hall? They practice, practice, practice. The orchestra becomes exceptional by using deliberate tactics, including practice, coaching, mentoring, formal training, exchange programs, and stretch assignments. The musicians' talent is only one small part of the process, the unwatered and uncultivated seed of excellence!

Your leadership development requires a similar approach. It starts with a clear understanding of what you are trying to accomplish, who is involved on your team, the values and mission of your organization, and a step-by-step plan to close your gaps and build on your strengths.

That's the beauty of the Innovative Leadership framework; it's a structured process you use to assess yourself now and plan how you want to grow. Because we're not prescriptive, our process is really more of a framework: highly flexible, proven effective, and able to adapt and incorporate components from specific leadership philosophies that fit your end goal. From "moving the cheese" to servant leadership, our process supports whatever index you choose. The Innovative Leadership framework doesn't just help you be you; it helps you be the best leader possible.

After identifying your development goals, it is vital to identify a support team to provide expertise, be accountability partners, and give feedback on progress. Support partners can help us think through whose jobs will change as we change and how we will practice new behaviors inside and outside of work. When considering who should be on your development team, consider developmental perspective, mindset, and availability; you want to be sure they model what you want to become, agree with your desire to grow, and have the time to help. Their methods should align with your style; for example, some people like to give and receive direct feedback. Others prefer gentle recommendations. The goal is to know each team member's style and craft explicit agreements to get what you need the way that works best for you. You may also want feedback from family members in addition to colleagues. When we change, we may need a safe place to practice new skills. Spouses, partners, roommates and close friends can provide safe relationships to practice before we "go live" using new skills at work.

Scorecards help monitor progress, but plans rarely go as expected. We often receive feedback or learn about an unintended consequence of our growth/ change that requires a revision to the plan. Set up a process to review and revise goals to reflect what you are learning about yourself (and your environment) as you develop.

Once you take action on your development plan and get feedback, you might shift your plan or your goals. You may experience a dynamic tension between what you want and the effort required to accomplish it in your timeline. It's okay to shift your timeline, change your action plan, or adjust your goals. This is a natural and healthy process of accomplishing lifelong learning objectives.

Lead: Be, Relate, and Do

Be

When defining your vision and values, set the foundation for who (vision) and how (values) you want to be. If you imagine the most influential leaders you admire, how would you describe their essence? That's what you want to.

Relate

Chapter 2 revealed the interconnections of effective leaders and followers. A leader's ability to relate to others across the following four psychosocial contexts creates an engaging and empowering environment:

- **Personal.** Connect with and be aware of your purpose, values, type, developmental perspective, resilience, mindsets, and competencies.

- **Interpersonal.** Relationships involving pairs of people include building trust and shared agreements about working together.

- **Team.** Your people and their work group's arrangements about how they will accomplish their work, including communication, accountabilities, and decision-making.

- **Organizational.** The vision, culture, systems, strategic initiatives, and impact measures are involved in a division, business unit, or organization.

These are particularly important as artificial intelligence continues to grow in the workplace. For a thriving workplace, your followers must know you relate to them as people, not machine tools.

Chapter 9 further defined the communication process, JEDI, virtuous character, and ESG. Each of these elements impacts how you relate with your followers, teams, and organization as well as external stakeholders.

How you relate makes the difference between your ability to inspire, motivate and engage or just tell people what to do. Truly exceptional leaders master the ability to relate to a diverse range of stakeholders.

Do

Innovative Leaders:

- **Set an inspirational vision** of success and guide the organization based on performance and the value of the organization's positive impact. Embody the vision you set through your being.

- **Leverage the team** for answers as part of the decision-making process.

- **Behave like a scientist**, continually experimenting, measuring, and testing for improvement and exploring new models and approaches.

- **Constantly learn** and develop self and others.

- **Motivate, inspire, and engage people** to perform through your leadership behaviors such as strategic focus, mentoring and coaching, and how you relate (i.e., emotional and social intelligence), your communication, JEDI actions, and virtuous character.

- **Pay attention to strategic goals and measures** like profit, customer satisfaction, employee engagement, community impact, and cultural cohesion.

- **Adapt to situations** and embrace new ideas, new approaches, and change.

- **Develop people and resources** to expand organizational capacity.

- **Create an environment of mutual support and integrity** that maximizes the employee experience by creating a vision that inspires employees to be their best selves including ensuring you are living your virtuous character, JEDI plans, and ESG goals.

Leadership development is often a challenging and humbling process. It requires you to identify your highest vision for yourself, as well as the gaps that will hold you back. This exploration requires you to look hard at facets of your thinking and behavior that you have outgrown and need to change and/or unlearn.

To recap: continually engage in a structured development process to meet your highest potential. This process allows you to identify what you believe and value and the impact you want to make in the world. You'll also craft a plan to develop the facets of your leadership that will significantly impact your ability to live to your highest potential. As you learned in each chapter, you can use AI tools to enhance your development process.

Using AI to Supplement Leadership Development

ALL ABOUT
AI

A core point of this chapter is that — as a leader — it's your responsibility to constantly evolve and improve your skills to better serve your organization and the people you lead. AI is the technology particularly suited to help you with that.

AI can identify improvement areas, provide personalized feedback, and recommend specific learning resources to help you grow. It can augment the processes outlined in this chapter, such as supplementing the assessment process with AI-driven evaluation tools. In a post-pandemic world, where remote work and digital transformation have become the norm, AI also helps you stay connected and engaged with your team, even (especially?) when you're not physically together. In particular, consider using:

- **Chatbots**, which can provide personalized coaching and feedback to you. For example, a chatbot could analyze your communication style and provide recommendations on being more effective in different situations, or with different followers.

- **Predictive analytics.** We mentioned its use in financial decisions in a previous chapter, but predictive analytics also help your development. By analyzing your communication skills, decision-making abilities, and emotional intelligence, AI can isolate areas where you may need to focus your development efforts.

- **Immersive learning experiences.** Virtual reality simulations have been around for years, most prominently in gaming. It's growing in education, too; in the workplace, this allows you to practice and refine your skills in a safe and controlled environment. This is especially useful for developing skills such as conflict resolution, where real-life practice can be challenging and holds a higher risk.

Of course, like any tool, AI is only as effective as the humans who create and use it. As a leader, you must intentionally use AI in your development efforts — but approach it as a supplement to, rather than a replacement for, human interaction and feedback. And always be mindful of the limitations of AI, such as the risk of bias and the potential for algorithms to perpetuate existing inequalities influencing their data.

Ultimately, the key to successful leadership development with AI is approaching it with an open mind and a willingness to learn. The more you know about AI and its potential for supporting leadership development, the more you can leverage its power to make yourself a better leader and your organization stronger.

REFLECTION QUESTIONS

- How would you describe your vision and values?

- How will you put your beliefs or attitudes into practice to optimize your impact?

- What is the most valuable insight you've learned from this book?

- How has this book changed your views on your organization's leadership? On leadership?

DIVE DEEPER

Articles

"How Busy People Can Develop Leadership Skills" by Darja Kragt (Harvard Business Review)

"How to Be a Purpose-Driven Leader without Burning Out" by Lisa Earle McLeod and Elizabeth Lotardo (Harvard Business Review)

Podcast Episodes

Innovating Leadership: Co-Creating Our Future
Season 8 Episode 1: "Do It on Purpose"

Innovating Leadership: Co-Creating Our Future
Season 9 Episode 5: "Leading with Care and Purpose"

Continue Your Innovative Leadership Journey

Well done on finishing this book! We hope it's been a transformative experience that's expanded your thinking about leadership — focusing not just on actions, but also on your overall attitude and relationships.

Throughout your journey, you dove into the Innovative Leadership framework, and learned how it equips you for today's rapidly evolving workplace. While we touched on the role of AI, remember: it's just one piece of a bigger puzzle. So, what's next?

Take a moment to revisit the reflection questions you answered earlier. How have your views shifted now that you've fully explored the Innovative Leadership framework? How do you see AI contributing to your growth as a leader? How can these new insights make you more effective in a tech-driven environment?

Also, don't forget to show appreciation for those who've helped you along the way. How do you plan to express your gratitude (in a manner befitting your culture, of course)? Is it time for a celebration with your support team? Whether it's a group huddle or individual thank-you notes, celebrate your progress.

As for sharing what you've learned, have you considered initiating a discussion group with your team or other stakeholders? It's a great way to continue growing together.

So go ahead — give yourself a pat on the back! You're one step closer to becoming a future-ready, innovative leader. Take time to celebrate both your achievements and the help you've received from others.

Cheers to your success!

REFERENCES

For our list of references and additional resources with clickable links, go to www.innovativeleadershipessentials.com.

Anderson, B., & Adams, C. D. (2016). *Mastering leadership: An integrated framework for breakthrough performance and extraordinary business results.* Wiley.

Antonakis, J., Fenley, M., & Liechti, S. (2011). Can charisma be taught? Tests of two interventions. *Academy of Management Learning & Education, 10*(3), 374–396.

Antonakis, J., Fenley, M., & Liechti, S. (2012). Learning charisma: Transform yourself into the person others want to follow. *Harvard Business Review, 90*(6), 127–130.

Austin, J. (2014). All that is needed for evil to triumph is for good people to say nothing—human factors in effective safety-conversation interventions. *The APPEA Journal, 54*(2), 508. https://doi.org/10.1071/aj13081

Banaji, M. R., & Greenwald, A. G. (2013). *Blindspot: Hidden biases of good people*. Delacorte Press.

Barry, E. S., & Grunberg, N. E. (2019). Healthcare teams. In J. F. Quinn & B. A. White (Eds.), *Cultivating leadership in medicine* (1st ed., pp. 117-130). Kendall Hunt Publishing Company.

Barry, E.S., & Grunberg, N.E. (2020). A conceptual framework to guide leader and follower education, development, and assessment. *Journal of Leadership, Accountability, and Ethics*. 17(1), 127-134. https://doi.org/10.33423/jlae.v17i1.2795

Barry, E., Grunberg, N., Metcalf, M., Morelli, C., & Morrow-Fox, M. (2022). Leading post-pandemic and beyond: Innovative leadership. *Cutter*. https://www.cutter.com/article/innovative-leadership-leading-post-pandemic-beyond

Baschuk, B. (2023, April 30). Tech, AI driving job changes for nearly a quarter of all workers. *Bloomberg*. https://www.bloomberg.com/news/articles/2023-04-30/tech-ai-driving-job-changes-for-nearly-a-quarter-of-all-workers?leadSource=uverify%20wall#xj4y7vzkg

Baschuk, B. (2023, May 3). Microsoft economist warns bad actors will use AI to cause damage. *Bloomberg*. https://www.bloomberg.com/news/articles/2023-05-03/ai-will-cause-real-damage-microsoft-chief-economist-warns#xj4y7vzkg

Bethlehem, R.A.I., Seidlitz, J., White, S.R. et al. Brain charts for the human lifespan. *Nature* 604, 525–533 (2022). https://doi.org/10.1038/s41586-022-04554-y

Boaz, N., & Fox, E. A. (2014). *Change leader, Change thyself*. (March 2014). McKinsey Quarterly.

Brown, B. (2011). *Conscious leadership for sustainability: How leaders with a late-stage action logic design and engage in sustainability initiatives* [Doctoral dissertation, Fielding Graduate University].

Bunin, J. L., Durning, S., & Weber, L. (2022). Harnessing followership to empower graduate medical education trainees. *Journal of Medical Education and Curricular Development*, 9, 23821205221096380. https://doi.org/10.1177/23821205221096380

Chaleff, I. (2009). *The courageous follower: Standing up to and for our leaders.* Berrett-Koehler Publishers.

Collins, J. (2001). *Good to great: Why some companies leap and others don't* (1st ed.). Harper Business.

Cook-Greuter, S. (2004). Making a case for a developmental perspective. *Industrial and Commercial Training, 36*(7), 275–281. https://doi.org/10.1108/00197850410563902

Covey, S. R. (1989). *The seven habits of highly effective people.* Free Press.

Crossan, M., Côté, S., & Virgin, S. (2020). You are elevating leader character alongside competence in selection. *Organizational Dynamics.* https://doi.org/10.1016/j.orgdyn.2020.100752

Crossan, M., Seijts, G., & Gandz, J. (2015). *Developing leadership character* (1st ed.). Routledge.

Cummings, J. P. (n.d.). Active listening: The leader's Rosetta Stone. *The Professional Bulletin of the Armor Branch, CXXI*(5), 38–42.

Dastin, J. (2018, October 10). Amazon scraps secret AI recruiting tool that showed bias against women. *Reuters.* https://www.reuters.com/article/us-amazon-com-jobs-automation-insight-idUSKCN1MK08G

Dinwoodie, D.L., Lewis, S., & Ritchie-Dunham, J. (2022). *Navegar por la incertidumbre y aprender con agilidad, claves en el trabajo del futuro* [Navigating Complexity and Learning with Agility: Keys for the Future of Work]. Harvard Duesto Business Review. https://www.harvard-deusto.com/navegar-por-la-incertidumbre-y-aprender-con-agilidad-claves-en-el-trabajo-del-futuro

Eliot, L. (2023, April 20). When you use ChatGPT you could be legally liable, AI ethics and law experts warn. *Forbes.* https://www.forbes.com/sites/lanceeliot/2023/04/10/when-you-use-chatgpt-you-could-be-legally-liable-ai-ethics and-law-experts-warn/?sh=4fa27f657c34

The Enneagram Institute. (2017). Enneagram. www.enneagraminstitute.com

Fisher-Borne, M., Cain, J., & Martin, S. (2015). From mastery to accountability: Cultural humility as an alternative to cultural competence. *Social Work Education, 34*(2), 165–181. https://doi.org/10.1080/02615479.2014.977244

Fitch, G., Ramirez, V., & O'Fallon, T. (2010). Enacting containers for integral transformative development. [Paper presentation]. Integral Theory Conference 2010, Pleasant Hill, CA.

Fowler, G. (2023, August 7). AI is acting 'pro-anorexia' and tech companies aren't stopping it. The Washington Post. https://www.washingtonpost.com/technology/2023/08/07/ai-eating-disorders-thinspo-anorexia-bulimia

Gallup (2023) State of the global workplace: 2023 report. *Gallup.* https://www.gallup.com/workplace/349484/state-of-the-global-workplace.aspx

Gates, B. (2023, March 28). Here's what the age of AI means for the world, According to Bill Gates. *World Economic Forum.* https://www.weforum.org/agenda/2023/03/heres-what-the-age-of-ai-means-for-the-world-according-to-bill-gates/#:~:text=The%20development%20of%20AI%20is,industries%20will%20reorient%20around%20it

Gauthier, A. (2008). Developing generative change leaders across sectors: An exploration of integral approaches. *Integral Leadership Review, 8*(1).

Goleman, D. (1995). *Emotional Intelligence.* Bantam Books.

Goleman, D. (1998). *Working with Emotional Intelligence.* Bantam Books.

Goleman, D., Boyatzis, R., & McKee, A. (2002). *Primal Leadership: Learning to Lead with Emotional Intelligence.* Harvard Business School Press.

Grunberg, N.E., Barry, E.S., Callahan, C.W., Kleber, H., McManigle, J.E., Schoomaker, E.B., (2018). A conceptual framework for leader and leadership education and development. *International Journal of Leadership in Education*, 22(5), 1-7. https://doi.org/10.1080/13603124.2018.1492026

Hofstede, G. (1980). *Culture's consequences: International differences in work-related values.* Sage Publications.

Howe-Murphy, R. revised and updated (2020). *Deep living with the enneagram: Recovering your true nature.* Enneagram Press.

Howe-Murphy, R., 2nd edition (2022). *Deep coaching: Using the enneagram as a catalyst for profound change.* Enneagram Press.

Howe-Murphy, R., (2023). *Underneath your personality: Discover greater well-being through deep living with the enneagram.* Enneagram Press.

Implicit Association Test (IAT). (2011). Project Implicit. https://implicit.harvard.edu/implicit/takeatest.html

Intriligator, J. (2023, July 21). Gliding, not searching: Here's how to reset your view of ChatGPT to steer it to better results. *The Conversation.* https://theconversation.com/gliding-not-searching-heres-how-to-reset-your-view-of-chatgpt-to-steer-it-to-better-results-205819

Kellerman, B. (2008). *Followership: How followers are creating change and changing leaders.* Harvard Business School Press Boston.

Kellerman, B. (2012). *The end of leadership.* Harper Collins.

Kelley, R. E. (1988). In praise of followers. *Harvard Business Review*, 66, 142-148.

Kelley, R. E. (2008). Rethinking followership. In R. E. Riggio, I. Chaleff, & J. Lipman-Blumen (Eds.), *The art of followership: How great followers create great leaders and organizations* (pp. 5-16). Jossey-Bass.

Kerns, C. D. (2016). High-impact communicating: A key leadership practice. *Journal of Applied Business and Economics, 18*(5), 11–22.

Klatt, M. D., Buckworth, J., & Malarkey, W. B. (2008). Effects of low-dose mindfulness-based stress reduction (mbsr-ld) on working adults. *Health Education & Behavior, 36*(3), 601–614. https://doi.org/10.1177/1090198108317627

Klippenstein, K. (2023, July 25). As actors strike for AI protections, Netflix lists $900,000 AI job. *The Intercept.* https://theintercept.com/2023/07/25/strike-hollywood-ai-disney-netflix

Kotter, J. P. (2012). *Leading change.* Harvard Business Review Press.

Laloux, F. (2014). *Reinventing organizations: A guide to creating organizations inspired by the next stage of human consciousness.* Nelson Parker.

Leadership Circle. (2022). *The Leadership Circle.* [Assessment]. https://leadershipcircle.com

Luthans, F., & Youssef, C. M. (2004). Human, social, and now positive psychological capital management: Investing in people for competitive advantage. *Organizational Dynamics, 33*(2), 143-160.

Maddi, S. R., & Khoshaba, D. M. (2005). *Resilience at Work: How to Succeed No Matter What Life Throws at You.* AMACOM Books.

Maslow, A. (1943). A theory of human motivation. *Psychological Review, 50*, 370-396.

Metcalf, M. (2008). Level 5 leadership: Leadership that transforms organizations and creates sustainable results. *Integral Leadership Review, 8*(1).

Metcalf, M. (2015, October 12). Leadership 2050 competency model. *Innovating Leadership Institute Insights.*

https://www.innovativeleadershipinstitute.com/leadership-2050-competency-model

Metcalf, M. (2016, August 30) What is the path for leadership maturity? *Forbes.* https://www.forbes.com/sites/forbescoachescouncil/2016/08/30/what-is-the-path-for-leadership-maturity/?sh=7ca84f7a1b6c

Metcalf, M. (2020, May 6). Seven Key Crisis Leadership Skills. *Forbes.* https://www.forbes.com/sites/forbescoachescouncil/2020/05/06/seven-key-crisis-leadership-skills/?sh=9bfaa3c790a3

Metcalf, M. (2020, August 27). Leading during a crisis: Retooling leadership. *Training Industry.* https://trainingindustry.com/articles/leadership/leading-during-a-crisis-retooling-leadership

Metcalf, M. (2021, October 11). Are you a future-ready leader? *Innovative Leadership Institute Insights.* https://www.innovativeleadershipinstitute.com/are-you-a-future-ready-leader

Metcalf, M. (2022) Innovative leadership: An ongoing development journey. *Forbes.* https://www.forbes.com/sites/forbescoachescouncil/2022/05/04/innovative-leadership-an-ongoing-development-journey/?sh=b93d9a75640a

Metcalf, M. (Host). (2022, December 15). The new role of leadership in a hybrid workplace. [Audio podcast episode]. In *Innovating leadership: Co-creating our future.* Innovative Leadership Institute. https://innovatingleadership.podbean.com/e/the-new-role-of-leadership-in-a-hybrid-workplace

Metcalf, M. (Host). (2023, January 18). Courageous followership. [Audio podcast episode]. In *Innovating leadership: Co-creating our future.* Innovative Leadership Institute. https://innovatingleadership.podbean.com/e/follow

Metcalf, M. (Host). (2023, February 27). Leadership 2050. [Audio podcast episode]. In *Innovating Leadership: Co-Creating Our Future.* Innovative Leadership Institute. https://iliarchive.podbean.com/e/leadership-2050

Metcalf, M. (Host). (2023, March 3). How does the brain impact leadership resilience? [Audio podcast episode]. In *Innovating Leadership: Co-Creating Our Future.* Innovative Leadership Institute. https://iliarchive.podbean.com/e/s4-ep36-how-does-the-brain-impact-leadership-resilience

Metcalf, M. (Host). (2023, March 14). What Does the Leader of the Future Really Look Like? [Audio podcast episode]. In *Innovating Leadership: Co-Creating Our Future.* Innovative Leadership Institute. https://iliarchive.podbean.com/e/s1-ep14-what-does-the-leader-of-the-future-really-look-like

Metcalf, M. (Host). (2023, March 20). Building leadership self-awareness using type. [Audio podcast episode]. In *Innovating leadership: Co-creating our future.* Innovative Leadership Institute. https://iliarchive.podbean.com/e/s3-ep17-building-leadership-self-awareness-using-type

Metcalf, M. (Host). (2023, March 20). Building resilience: A key foundation for change [Audio podcast episode]. In *Innovating Leadership: Co-Creating Our Future.* Innovative Leadership Institute. https://iliarchive.podbean.com/e/s3-ep32-building-resilience-a-key-foundation-for-change

Metcalf, M. (Host). (2023, March 23). The dance between leadership and followership. [Audio podcast episode]. In *Innovating leadership: Co-creating our future.* Innovative Leadership Institute. https://iliarchive.podbean.com/e/s4-ep9-the-dance-between-leadership-and-followership

Metcalf, M. (Host). (2023, March 23). Organizational development: understanding human development. [Audio podcast episode]. In *Innovating leadership: Co-creating our future.* Innovative Leadership Institute. https://iliarchive.podbean.com/e/s4-ep14-organizational-development-understanding-human-development

Metcalf, M. (Host). (2023, March 23). Using enneagram assessment to build leadership effectiveness. [Audio podcast episode]. In *Innovating leadership: Co-creating our future.* Innovative Leadership Institute. https://iliarchive.podbean.com/e/s4-ep20-using-enneagram-assessment-to-build-leadership-effectiveness

Metcalf, M. (Host). (2023, April 10). How developmental maturity aligns with organizational maturity. [Audio podcast episode]. In *Innovating leadership: Co-creating our future.* Innovative Leadership Institute. https://iliarchive.podbean.com/e/s4-ep38-how-developmental-maturity-aligns-with-organizational-maturity

Metcalf, M. (2023, April 28). Unlocking your leadership potential: A guide to harnessing generative AI. *Innovative Leadership Institute Insights.* https://www.innovativeleadershipinstitute.com/unlocking-your-leadership-potential-a-guide-to-harnessing-generative-ai

Metcalf, M. (Host). (2023, May 31). Unleashing the power of human-AI collaboration. [Audio podcast episode]. In *Innovating leadership: Co-creating our future.* Innovative Leadership Institute. https://innovatingleadership.podbean.com/e/aipower

Metcalf, M., Morrow-Fox, M., Stoller, J., Pfeil, S., Souba, W. (2014). *Innovative leadership workbook for physician leaders.* Integral Publishers.

Morrow-Fox, M., & Metcalf, M. (2020). Business Agility. *Integral Leadership Review, 20*(1), 78–80.

Nolan, C. (Director). (2022). *It's VUCA: The secret to living in the 21st century* [Film]. 90,000 Feet.

Northouse, P. G. (2010). *Leadership: Theory and Practice.* Sage Publications.

O'Fallon, T., Fitch, G., & Carman, D. (2008, August 7–10). *Experiments in second-tier community: Collective individualism.* [Paper presentation]. First Integral Theory Conference, Pleasant Hill, CA, United States.

O'Fallon, T., Polissar, N., Neradilek, M., & Murray, T. (2020). The validation of a new scoring method for assessing ego development based on three dimensions of language. *Heliyon, 6*(3), e03472. https://doi.org/10.1016/j.heliyon.2020.e03472

Ortiz, S. (2023, July 19). GPT-4 is getting significantly dumber over time, according to a study. *ZDNET.* https://www.zdnet.com/article/gpt-4-is-getting-significantly-dumber-over-time-according-to-a-study

Patel, A., & Plowman, S. (2022, August 17). The increasing importance of a best friend at work. *Gallup.* https://www.gallup.com/workplace/397058/increasing-importance-best-friend-work.aspx

Pronin, E. (2007). Perception and misperception of bias in human judgment. *Trends in Cognitive Sciences, 11*(1), 37–43. https://doi.org/10.1016/j.tics.2006.11.001

Ritchie-Dunham, J. L. (2014) *Ecosynomics: The science of abundance.* Vibrancy Publishing.

Richmer, H. R. (2011). *An analysis of the effects of enneagram-based leader development on self-awareness: A case study at a Midwest utility company* (UMI Number: 3629159) [Doctoral dissertation, Spalding University]. Proquest.

Rock, D. (2008). SCARF: A brain-based model for collaborating with and influencing others. *NeuroLeadership Journal, 1*, 1–9.

Rock, D. (2009, August 27). Managing with the brain in mind. *Strategy + business. 2009*(56).

Rooke, D. & Torbert, W.R. (2005, April). Seven transformations of leadership. *Harvard Business Review.* https://hbr.org/2005/04/seven-transformations-of-leadership

Sowcik, M. (2015). *Leadership 2050: Critical challenges, key contexts, and emerging trends (building leadership bridges)* (4th ed.). Emerald Publishing Limited.

STAGES International. (2023). STAGES model. https://www.stagesinternational.com/stagesassessments

Switzler, A., Grenny, J., Patterson, K., & McMillan, R. (2002). *Crucial conversations: Tools for talking when stakes are high* (2nd ed.). McGraw Hill.

Terrell, S. (2020). *Learning mindset for leaders: Leveraging experience to accelerate development.* Independently Published.

Tervalon, M., & Murray-Garcia, J. (1998). Cultural humility versus cultural competence: A critical distinction in defining physician training outcomes in multicultural education. *Journal of Health Care for the Poor and Underserved, 9*(2), 117–125.

Titareva, T. (2021, February 5). *Leadership in an artificial intelligence era.* [Paper presentation]. Leading Change Conference 2021, James Madison University. https://commons.lib.jmu.edu/cgi/viewcontent.cgi?article=1012&context=leadcc

Torbert, W. R., Cook-Greuter, S., Fisher, D., Foldy, E., Gauthier, A., & Keeley, J. (2004). *Action inquiry: The secret of timely and transformational leadership.* Berrett-Koehler.

Ungar, M. (2011). *The social ecology of resilience: A handbook of theory and practice.* Springer.

Wardini, J. (2023, July 26). 101 artificial intelligence statistics [updated for 2023]. *Techjury.* https://techjury.net/blog/ai-statistics

Washington, C. (2022, August 3). Innovative leadership: Moving beyond resilience to antifragility. *Innovative Leadership Institute Insights.* https://www.innovativeleadershipinstitute.com/innovative-leadership-moving-beyond-resilience-to-antifragility

Whelan, T., Atz, U., Van Holt, T., & Clark, C. (2020). ESG and financial performance:

Uncovering the relationship between ESG and financial performance through meta-analysis of 1,000+ studies. NYU Stern Center for Sustainable Business. https://www.stern.nyu.edu/sites/default/files/assets/documents/NYU-RAM_ESG-Paper_2021%20Rev_0.pdf

World Economic Forum (2023). *Future of jobs report: 2023.* [White paper]. World Economic Forum. https://www3.weforum.org/docs/WEF_Future_of_Jobs_2023.pdf

ADDITIONAL RESOURCES:

Books, Articles, and Audio Files:

Ahearn, B. (2019). *Influence people: Powerful everyday opportunities to persuade that are lasting and ethical.* Influence People, LLC.

Bradberry, T., & Greaves, J. (2009). *Emotional intelligence 2.0.* TalentSmart.

Braks, A. J. (2020). *Executive coaching in strategic holistic leadership: The drivers and dynamics of vertical development.* Open University Press.

Brown, B. (2013). *The future of leadership for conscious capitalism* [White paper]. http://www.metaintegralstore.com

Csikszentmihalyi, M. (2008). *Flow: The psychology of optimal experience* (1st ed.). Harper Perennial Modern Classics.

Ford, J. (2020). *Hijacked by your brain.* Sourcebooks.

Ford, J., & Ford, L. (2009). *The four conversations: Daily communication that gets results* (1st ed.). Berrett-Koehler Publishers.

Gibbons, P. (2015). *The science of successful organizational change: How leaders set strategy, change behavior, and create an agile culture* (1st ed.). Pearson FT Press.

Heifetz, R. A., Linsky, M., & Grashow, A. (2009). *The practice of adaptive leadership: Tools and tactics for changing your organization and the world* (1st ed.). Harvard Business Press.

Howe-Murphy, R. (2023) *Underneath Your Personality: Discover Greater Well-Being Through Deep Living with the Enneagram.* Enneagram Press.

Howe-Murphy, R. (2013). *Deep living: Transforming your relationship to everything that matters through the enneagram.* Enneagram Press.

Howe-Murphy, R. (2007). *Deep coaching: Using the enneagram as a catalyst for profound change.* Enneagram Press.

Hudson, R., Riso, D. R. (1999). *The wisdom of the enneagram: The complete guide to psychological and spiritual growth for the nine personality types.* Bantam Books.

Hunt, V., Layton, D., & Prince, S. (2015, January 1) Why diversity matters. McKinsey & Company. https://www.mckinsey.com/capabilities/people-and-organizational-performance/our-insights/why-diversity-matters

What is diversity, equity, and inclusion? (2022, August 17). *McKinsey & Company.* https://www.mckinsey.com/featured-insights/mckinsey-explainers/what-is-diversity-equity-and-inclusion?stcr=78BC983D06464AAA862C0DE9993B8B4B&cid=other-eml-alt-mip-mck&hlkid=6ef62e307c4e4c3da5bcdb07df19cf07&hctky=14818134&hdpid=b5f5b88b-74b6-4cd6-9c5d-4fb4e258863d#

Johnson, B. (2014). *Polarity management: Identifying and managing unsolvable problems*. H R D Press.

Leitch, J., Rooke, D., Wilson, R., Lancefield, D., & Dawson, M. (2015). *The hidden talent: Ten ways to identify and retain transformational leaders*. PwC.

Leonard, G., & Murphy, M. (1995). *The life we are given: A long-term program for realizing the potential of body, mind, heart, and soul* (1st ed.). G. P. Putnam's Sons.

Metcalf, M., & Palmer, M. (2011). *Innovative leadership Fieldbook*. Integral Publishers.

Metcalf, M., & Paluck, D. (2010). The story of Jill– How an individual leader developed into a "Level 5" leader. *Integral Leadership Review, 10*(3).

Metcalf, M., & Ritchie-Dunham, J. (2016). Co-hosting: Creating optimal experience for team interactions. *Integral Leadership Review, 16*(3).

Metcalf, M. (Host). (2022, October 28). Leveraging creative conflict to improve impact. [Audio podcast episode]. In *Innovating leadership: Co-creating our future*. Innovative Leadership Institute. https://classcontent.podbean.com/e/leveraging-creative-conflict-to-improve-impact

Metcalf, M. (Host). (2022, November 1). Digital body language: How to build trust and connection. [Audio podcast episode]. In *Innovating leadership: Co-creating our future*. Innovative Leadership Institute. https://classcontent.podbean.com/e/digital-body-language-how-to-build-trust-and-connection

Metcalf, M. (Host). (2022, November 1). Leading with story: Captivate, convince, inspire. [Audio podcast episode]. In *Innovating leadership: Co-creating our future*. Innovative Leadership Institute. https://classcontent.podbean.com/e/paul-smith-leading-with-story-captivate-convince-inspire

Metcalf, M. (Host). (2022, December 15). Stewarding the future of the planet: Views from the boardroom. [Audio podcast episode]. In *Innovating leadership: Co-creating our future*. Innovative Leadership Institute. https://innovatingleadership.podbean.com/e/dei-in-the-boardroom-diverse-leadership-is-better-business

Metcalf, M. (Host). (2022, December 19). Leading with character: A real-life red roof report. [Audio podcast episode]. In *Innovating leadership: Co-creating our future*. Innovative Leadership Institute. https://innovatingleadership.podbean.com/e/leading-with-character-a-real-life-red-roof-report

Metcalf, M. (Host). (2023, March 6). Evolve to execute: Leadership maturity. [Audio podcast episode]. In *Innovating leadership: Co-creating our future*. Innovative Leadership Institute. https://iliarchive.podbean.com/e/s5-ep49-evolve-to-execute-leadership-maturity

Metcalf, M. (Host). (2023, May 23). You belong: LinkedIn brings diversity & inclusion home. [Audio podcast episode]. In *Innovating leadership: Co-creating our future*. Innovative Leadership Institute. https://innovatingleadership.podbean.com/e/linkedin

Ritchie-Dunham, J. L. (2014). *Ecosynomics: The science of abundance.* Vibrancy Ins, LLC.

Russell, T. (2015). *Mindfulness in motion: Unlock the secrets of mindfulness in motion.* Watkins Publishing.

Scharmer, O. (2016). *Theory u: Leading from the future as it emerges* (2nd ed.). Berrett-Koehler Publishers.

Senge, P. M. (1994). *The fifth discipline fieldbook: Strategies and tools for building a learning organization* (Illustrated ed.). Currency.

Sinek, S. (2019). *The infinite game.* Penguin.

Sinek, S. (2014). *Leaders eat last: Why some teams pull together, and others don't.* Portfolio.

Tsipursky, G. (2019). *Never go with your gut: How pioneering leaders make the best decisions and avoid business disasters (avoid terrible advice, cognitive biases, and poor decisions).* Career Press.

ASSESSMENT INSTRUMENTS:*

Emotional Intelligence Test: https://globalleadershipfoundation.com/geit/eitest.html

Enneagram (for Leader Type): www.enneagraminstitute.com

Extended DISC Instrument: https://www.extendeddisc.org

HeartMath®Tools for Reducing Stress and Staying Balanced: www.heartmath.org.

Implicit Association Test (IAT). (2011). Project Implicit. https://implicit.harvard.edu/implicit/takeatest.html

Innovative Leadership Institute Leadership Behavior Assessment: https://www.innovativeleadershipinstitute.com/what-we-do/leader-assessment.html (To order, send an email to inquiries@innovativeleadership.com)

Leadership Circle Profile: https://leadershipcircle.com/leadership-assessment-tools/leadership-circle-profile

Make Stress Good for You: https://www.hprc-online.org/mental-fitness/sleep-stress/make-stress-good-you

Mature Adult Profile Assessment (MAP; for a developmental perspective): http://www.verticaldevelopment.com/what-we-do/ (To order the MAP send an email to Map@verticaldevelopment.com)

NEO Personality Inventory-Revised: https://www.parinc.com/Products/Pkey/276

Perceived Stress Scale: http://www.mindgarden.com/documents/PerceivedStressScale.pdf

Position Success Indicator: https://www.positionsuccess.com

Resilience Assessment: https://innovativeleadershipinstitute.mykajabi.com/Resilienceduringdisruption and http://www.innovativeleadershipinstitute.com/resilience-assessment-tool.html

STAGES Model (for developmental perspective): https://www.stagesinternational.com/stagesassessments

StageSHIFT Vertical Holistic Leadership Profile: https://www.stageshift.coach/profile

*Some instruments require payment and/or a certified facilitator to provide feedback.

ABOUT THE AUTHORS

Maureen Metcalf

Maureen Metcalf is a highly respected executive advisor and the visionary founder and Chief Executive Officer of the Innovative Leadership Institute. Committed to creating a better world through exceptional leadership, Maureen guides her clients in elevating the quality of their leadership talent pool.

Recognized as a Fellow of the esteemed International Leadership Association, Maureen is also an accomplished author. Her international award-winning book series on Innovative Leadership, including the acclaimed *Innovative Leadership for Health Care*, received the prestigious International Book Award.

Beyond her writing achievements, Maureen extends her influence through her captivating international podcast, *Innovating Leadership: Co-Creating our Future*, ranked in the top 1% of podcasts globally. As the host, she leads engaging discussions on cutting-edge leadership practices, garnering a wide and appreciative audience.

Maureen's expertise is highly sought after in leadership, as evidenced by her regular contributions as a writer and expert contributor to Forbes.com. Her esteemed Forbes Coaches Council membership further solidifies her role as a trusted authority in the field.

With a passion for education, Maureen has shared her knowledge to students across various universities as an esteemed educator. She serves as the Vice President of James Madison University's School of Strategic Leadership Studies Advisory Committee and Franklin University's Mason Leadership Center, demonstrating her commitment to advancing the study and practice of strategic leadership, where she earned an honorary Doctorate.

Erin S. Barry

Erin S. Barry is an Assistant Professor in the Department of Anesthesiology at the Uniformed Services University (USU). She is a health professions education researcher who develops and delivers curriculum and education assessments and conducts research and scholarship related to leadership, followership, and healthcare teams. She has a secondary appointment as an Assistant Professor in the USU Department of Military and Emergency Medicine as well as the Center for Health Professions Education. She contributes to leadership education, development, assessment, scholarship, and online learning. Additionally, she is a Leadership Coach with certification from the Kansas Leadership Center and the Innovative Leadership Institute.

Ms. Barry earned a B.E. (2006) in Biomedical Engineering with a minor in Mathematics from Vanderbilt University in Nashville, TN. She earned an M.S. (2008) in Biomedical Engineering from University of Texas at Arlington with a focus on Tissue Engineering and Drug Delivery. She has worked at USU since 2010, where her research has focused on traumatic brain injury (TBI), post-traumatic stress disorder (PTSD), and leadership. She has co-authored more than 50 papers and chapters, as well as the book . She is a co-founder of the International Leadership Association's Healthcare Leadership Community. In addition, she helps to mentor faculty, staff, and students with regard to research activities. She is currently working on her Ph.D. in Health Professions Education, focusing on leadership and followership within healthcare teams.

Dan Mushalko

Dan Mushalko is Vice President for Media & Research with the Innovative Leadership Institute, where he produces and edits, a top leadership podcast (and ranked in the top 0.5% of podcasts worldwide). He is also a leadership course facilitator for Institute clients and co-leads a leadership course with ILI founder/CEO Maureen Metcalf for James Madison University. He has earned several leadership certifications from ILI. He is also certified as a VUCA Max Warrior coach.

Dan's career has been a continual weaving of writing, science, media, and leadership. He was the assistant editor of his university humor magazine, an in-house copywriter for an East Coast ad agency while studying applied physics, a scriptwriter for a national science-based radio adventure series, wrote and hosted an award-winning radio science show, taught creative writing, performed as a supplemental science teacher and presenter for school districts, and has spoken and guest-lectured on writing, science, and science fiction at conventions, seminars, university classes, and national meetings for science associations. He has also held management/leadership positions in organizations of all sizes.

His awards for science writing include best feature reporting from New Jersey's Society of Professional Journalists and the prestigious Westinghouse Science Journalism Award from the American Association for the Advancement of Science.

Devon Mushalko

Devon Mushalko is a Project Manager and Media Associate at the Innovative Leadership Institute. Having joined the Institute in 2021 as a media intern, Devon grew into her full-time position in 2023, where she now leads several projects across the organization. Among other duties, she currently serves as assistant editor and promotional content lead on the *Innovating Leadership: Co-Creating Our Future* podcast, develops the Institute's monthly Digest newsletter, and heads the experimental AI avatar project known as "FauxMo."

Devon honed her editorial skills as an intern with Thurber House, working on their *Teen Literary Journal*, and continues to practice those skills in a multitude of textual materials for the Institute, including blog posts, social media posts, marketing materials, and more. For *Innovative Leadership & Followership in the Age of AI*, Devon served as editor, proofreader, synthesizer, and reference checker.

Devon holds a Bachelor of Arts degree in English Literature with a minor in music from The Ohio State University (2020), has earned leadership development certifications from the Innovative Leadership Institute and the Global Leadership Mindset Development Program, and is a member of the International Leadership Association.

Neil E. Grunberg, Ph.D.

Neil E. Grunberg, Ph.D., is Professor of Military & Emergency Medicine and Professor of Neuroscience in the Uniformed Services University (USU) School of Medicine; Professor in the USU Graduate School of Nursing; and Director of Research and Development in the USU Leadership Education and Development (LEAD) program, Bethesda, Maryland. He also serves as the Director of Faculty Development for the Department of Military and Emergency Medicine and as the Chair, Faculty Mentoring and Development, Department of Anesthesiology. He is a medical psychologist, social psychologist, and behavioral neuroscientist.

Dr. Grunberg earned baccalaureate degrees in Medical Microbiology and Psychology from Stanford University (1975); M.A. (1977), M.Phil. (1979), and Ph.D. (1980) degrees in Physiological Psychology and Social Psychology from Columbia University; and completed doctoral training in Pharmacology at Columbia University's College of Physicians & Surgeons (1976-79).

He has been educating physicians, psychologists, and nurses for the Armed Forces and Public Health Service and scientists for research and academic positions since 1979. He has published > 220 papers addressing behavioral medicine, drug use, stress, traumatic brain injury, and leadership. He has been recognized for his professional contributions by awards from the American Psychological Association, Centers for Disease Control & Prevention, Food & Drug Administration, National Cancer Institute, Society for Behavioral Medicine, US Surgeon General, and Uniformed Services University. In 2015, Dr. Grunberg was selected to be a Presidential Leadership Scholar. He is a co-founder of the Healthcare Leadership Community of the International Leadership Association and a co-founder of the World Health Leadership Network. He also is a member of Teaching Followers Courage.

CONTRIBUTING AUTHORS

Michael Morrow-Fox, M.B.A., ED.S.

Michael Morrow-Fox, is a consultant with the Innovative Leadership Institute and is experienced in health care, education, banking, government, and non-profit management.

Michael has over 20 years of experience in leading technology and human resources operations and several years of full-time university teaching. He uses this background to blend his real-world understanding with current theoretical models helping his clients reach goals beyond their current thinking.

Michael has experience managing a 50-million-dollar technology budget, helping a technology startup company get off the ground, overseeing an international nonprofit organization achieve 'best place to work' status, and leading organizational education for a city government. His strengths are not in what area he works but in how he helps others work. Michael's project management, process excellence, problem-solving, and human performance management skills help companies form truly innovative strategies.

Michael has served as a full-time university faculty at Capital University, winning a Department of Education FIPSE Grant and the George Mason Program Excellence Award. He also served as the Director of Technology Strategy for OhioHealth Hospitals, as the Vice President of Operations for a technology start-up serving American Express, as the Vice President of Talent Management Training and Development for the American Heart Association, and the Manager of Organizational Education for the City of Greensboro, North Carolina. He has held Project Management Professional (PMP) Certification since 2002, has worked on Six Sigma Black Belt initiatives since 1999, and has been a Six Sigma Green Belt since 2006. His bachelor's degree focused on Industrial Psychology and Employee Counseling, his M.B.A. focus was on Organizational Leadership, his Educational Specialist Degree is in Educational Leadership, and Michael is working on his Doctoral dissertation in Educational Leadership.

Neil Sahota

Neil Sahota (萨冠军) is the CEO of ACSI Labs, United Nations (UN) AI Advisor, IBM Master Inventor, part-time Professor at UC Irvine, and author of best seller, *Own the A.I. Revolution*. With 20+ years of business experience, he works with organizations to create their core business strategy, enter new markets, and develop next generation products/solutions powered by emerging technology. His work experience spans multiple industries including legal services, healthcare, life sciences, retail, travel and transportation, energy and utilities, automotive, telecommunications, media/communication, and government. Moreover, Neil is one of the few people selected for IBM's Corporate Service Corps leadership program that pairs leaders with NGOs to perform community-driven economic development projects. For his assignment, Neil lived and worked in Ningbo, China where he partnered with Chinese corporate CEOs to create a leadership development program.

In addition, Neil partners with entrepreneurs to define their products, establish their target markets, and structure their companies. He is a member of several investor groups like the Tech Coast Angels, advises venture capital funds like Miramar and CerraCap, and helped create the UN's Innovation Factory, a global program for social impact entrepreneurs. Neil also serves as a judge in various startup competitions and mentor in several incubator/accelerator programs.

He actively pursues social good and volunteers with nonprofits. Neil cofounded the UN's AI for Good Initiative and is actively helping them building out their ecosystem of strategic partnerships. He is currently helping the Zero Abuse Project prevent child sexual abuse as well as Planet Home to engage youth culture in sustainability initiatives. Over the last twelve years, he has served as a Board Director to several non-profit organizations such as the Inteleos and Computing for Humanity as well as corporate boards from around the world like Legalmation, Lingmo, and Shineville.

THANK YOU FOR READING!

We appreciate your time and commitment in exploring the pages of *Innovative Leadership & Followership in the Age of AI*. The frameworks and reflection questions you've engaged with will contribute to your journey toward becoming a more effective leader, follower, and AI ally.

We understand that growth is a continuous and interconnected process, so we enthusiastically invite your valuable suggestions. We're open to receiving additional tools and templates that you may find beneficial, too.

If you'd like to connect with us, reach out through the Innovative Leadership Institute via email: **innovativeleadershipai@innovateleader.com**.

This guide marks the eleventh installment in our book series.
To access more resources and titles on Innovative Leadership, please visit **www.innovativeleadershipfieldbook.com.**

Thank you once again for your dedication to enhancing your leadership skills. We look forward to hearing from you, any insights or ideas you have — and most importantly, learning how your leadership journey progresses!